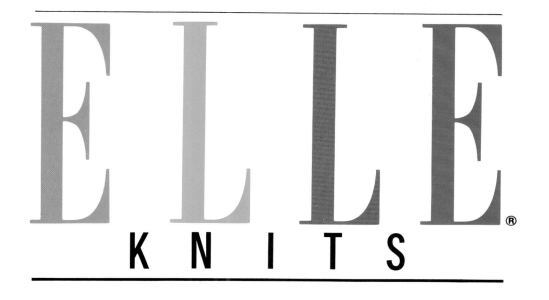

ELLE

Ballantine Books · New York

Library of Congress Catalog Card Number: 86-90718

ISBN: 0-345-33709-3

Manufactured in Spain

First American Edition: August 1986

10 9 8 7 6 5 4 3 2 1

Contents

Introduction

Knitting is an ancient craft that has recently taken on a new lease of life. The dreary patterns and drab yarns of some years ago have given way to a sudden flood of creative ideas and innovative designs. At the same time there has been an extraordinary wave of technical innovation in the matter of new yarns and knitting materials. Contemporary designers have made abundant use of these materials but they have also, on the whole, rejected much of the complex shaping and intricacy of traditional knitting design in favour of bold shapes, interesting colour patterns and simple stitches. So knitting has become more exciting but also easier and less daunting for beginners in the craft.

Elle magazine, which has been essential monthly reading for thousands of French women for many years has, as one would expect, been in the forefront of this revolution in knitting habits. The French, in any case, have a long tradition of combining style and simplicity in knitting as in other domestic crafts and the patterns in this book, all first published in *Elle*, have that casual understated elegance that is the hallmark of French fashion.

There are fifty patterns in the following pages, ranging from very simple styles suitable for beginners to garments with more complicated stitch patterns or shaping, which will provide something more challenging for experienced knitters. All the patterns, which include men's and children's wear as well as women's garments, are rated according to their degree of difficulty with one, two or three stars. In addition, they are divided into seasonal groupings, although these should not be taken as hard-and-fast categories. For example, a 'summer' style made in cotton could be a highly suitable winter garment if made in a woollen yarn.

The patterns have been translated and entirely rewritten using both metric and standard measurements. On page 121 American knitters will also find some notes and charts to help them with terminology and yarn equivalents, which will enable them to follow the patterns quite easily. The abbreviations used in the patterns are explained below. In some cases there may be special abbreviations that are relevant to one particular pattern only and these are given on the same page as the pattern itself.

The yarns used in the original patterns were all French and many of them are unobtainable, or obtainable outside France only in a few specialist shops. For those who may be able to find them, a list of these yarns is given on page 126 but otherwise the yarns quoted in the patterns are described in general terms only as 'double knitting', 'four ply', and so on. While this does allow you to choose among the huge range of wonderful yarns on the market, it also means that the choice must be exercised with more than the usual caution. Advice on choosing and buying yarn for these patterns is given on page 118. It is essential to read this very carefully before making a purchase. Before beginning work on any pattern it is also advisable to consult the section beginning on page 120, where guidance on following the patterns and, in particular, on reading colour and stitch pattern charts will be found. Where, as here, the yarns quoted are not branded ones, it is doubly important to make scrupulous tension checks. Do not embark on any pattern until you are absolutely sure that you have matched your tension to that specified in the pattern. Information on measuring and checking tension is given on page 122.

Abbreviations

alt – alternate(ly)
approx – approximately
beg – begin(ning)
cm – centimetre(s)
cont – continu(e)(ing)
dec – decreas(e)(es)(ing)
foll – follow(s)(ing)
g – gram(s)
g st – garter stitch
in – inch(es)
inc – increas(e)(es)(ing)
K – knit
K up – pick up and knit
K-wise – knitwise, as if to knit
LH – left-hand
m – metre(s)
mm – millimetres
oz – ounces
P – purl
patt – pattern
psso – pass slipped stitch over

P up – pick up and purl
P-wise – purlwise, as if to purl
p2sso – pass 2 slipped stitches over
rem – remain(s)(ing)
rep – repeat(s)
RH – right-hand
RS – right side
sl – slip
st(s) – stitch(es)
st st – stocking stitch (stockinette stitch)
tbl – through the back of the loop
tog – together
WS – wrong side
ybk – yarn between the needles to back of work
yd – yard(s)
yfwd – yarn forward (yarn over or yarn to front)
yon – yarn over needle (yarn over)
yrn – yarn round needle (yarn over)

STAR RATINGS

Easy to make, suitable for beginners

More difficult, for knitters with some experience

Challenging, requires expert skills for a perfect finish

Oatmeal

A straightforward cotton top with a homespun look. It's knitted in a fancy cotton yarn in an attractive slipstitch pattern.

SIZES
To fit 81[86,91]cm (32[34,36]in) bust

MATERIALS
300[350,400]g (11[13,15]oz) double knitting yarn
1 pair 4mm (US6) and 5mm (US8) needles

TENSION
22 sts and 38 rows to 10cm (4in) over slipstitch patt on 5mm (US8) needles.

FRONT
Using 4mm (US6) needles, cast on 106[110,114] sts.
Work 3 rows g st as foll:
Next row K to end.
Rep last row twice more.
Change to 5mm (US8) needles and commence slipstitch patt:
1st row (RS) K to end.
2nd row *K1, sl 1 P-wise; rep from * to last 2 sts, K2.
3rd row K to end.
4th row K2, *sl 1 P-wise, K1; rep from * to end.
These 4 rows form the slipstitch patt rep.
Cont in patt until work measures 26[27,28]cm (10[10½,11]in) from cast-on edge, ending with a WS row.
Shape armholes
Cast off 3 sts at beg of next 2 rows and then cast off 2 sts at beg of foll 10 rows. 80[84,88] sts.**
Work 4 rows straight.
Divide for neck
Next row Patt 38[40,42] sts, turn, leaving rem sts on a spare needle and cont on these sts only for first side of front.
Work straight until front measures 14cm (5½in) from beg of armhole shaping, ending at neck edge.
Shape neck
Cast off 8 sts at beg of next row, then 4 sts at beg of foll alt row and 3 sts at beg of next alt row.
Work 1 row.
Cast off 2 sts at beg of next row, and then dec 1 st at beg of foll 3 alt rows. 18[20,22] sts.
Work straight until front measures 20[21,22]cm (8[8¼,8½]in) from beg of armhole shaping, ending at armhole edge.
Cast off.
With RS facing, rejoin yarn to sts left on spare needle, cast off 4 sts, work in slipstitch patt to end.
Complete second side of neck to match first side, reversing shapings.

BACK
Work as given for the front of the sweater to **.
Work straight until back measures 4 rows less than front to shoulder, ending with a WS row.
Divide for neck
Next row Patt 28[30,32] sts, turn, leaving rem sts on a spare needle and cont on these sts only for first side of neck.
Cast off 10 sts at beg of next row.
Work straight until back matches front to shoulder.
Cast off.
With RS of work facing, rejoin yarn to sts left on spare needle, cast off 24 sts, patt to end.
Complete second side of back neck to match first side of back neck, reversing shaping.

SLEEVES
Using 4mm (US6) needles, cast on 58[62,66] sts.
Work 3 rows g st.
Change to 5mm (US8) needles and cont in patt as given for front, *at the same time* inc 1 st at each end of every foll 5th[5th,6th] row until there are 72[76,80] sts.
Now inc 1 st at each end of every foll 3rd[4th,4th] row until there are 86[90,94] sts.
Work straight until sleeve measures 18[19,20]cm (7[7½,8]in) from cast-on edge.
Shape top
Dec 1 st at each end of next and every foll alt row until there are 64[68,72] sts on needle.
Cast off.

MAKING UP
Darn in all ends neatly.
Join shoulder seams.
Neckband
Using 4mm (US6) needles, with RS of work facing, K up 104 sts evenly around neck edge.
Work 6 rows g st.
Cast off.
Front neckbands
Using 4mm (US6) needles, with RS of work facing, K up 33 sts along RH side of front opening.
Work 6 rows g st.
Cast off.
Work a similar band of 6 rows g st on LH side.
Overlap front neckbands and catch down base on WS.
Join side and sleeve seams.
Set in sleeves.

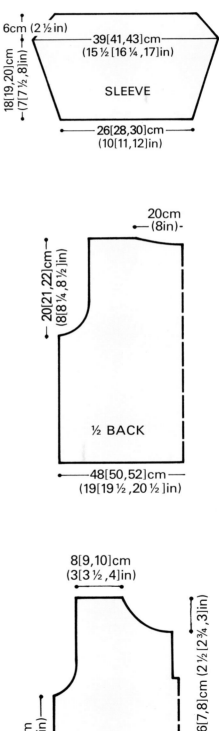

Designed by Valérie Ribadeau Dumas Photograph: Denis Boussard

Riviera

A lightly textured stitch pattern and a slubby cotton and linen yarn add an original touch to a conventional classic. For a winter version, make it in warm Aran wool.

SIZES
To fit chest 96[101,106]cm (38[40,42]in)

MATERIALS
1200[1300,1400]g (43[46,50]oz) Aran-weight yarn
1 pair each 4mm (US6) and 5mm (US8) needles

TENSION
19 sts and 22 rows to 10cm (4in) over patt on 5mm (US8) needles.

FRONT
Using 4mm (US6) needles, cast on 91[95,99] sts.
Work in twisted K1, P1 rib as foll:
1st row (RS) K1 tbl, *P1, K1 tbl; rep from * to end.
2nd row P1, *K1 tbl, P1; rep from *.
Rep these 2 rows for 8cm (3in), ending with a RS row.
Change to 5mm (US8) needles.
Next row P to end, inc 12 sts evenly across row. 103[107,111] sts.
Work in mock cable patt as foll:
1st row (RS) *P1, K into 2nd st on LH needle, then into 1st st, dropping both sts off needle at the same time; rep from * to last 1[2,0] sts, P to end.
2nd row P to end.
These 2 rows form the patt rep.
Cont in patt until work measures 34[35,36]cm (13½[13¾,14]in) from top of rib, ending with a WS row.
Shape armholes
Cast off 6 sts at beg of next 2 rows and 3 sts at beg of foll 4 rows. 79[83,87] sts.**
Now work straight until front measures 14[15,16]cm (5½[6,6¼]in) from beg of armhole shaping, ending with a WS row.
Divide for neck
Next row Patt 32[34,36] sts, turn, leaving rem sts on a spare needle and cont on these sts only for left side of neck.
Cast off 5 sts at beg of next row, 3 sts at beg of foll alt row, 2 sts at beg of next alt row and 1 st at beg of foll 3 alt rows, ending with a WS row. 19[21,23] sts.
Shape shoulder
Cast off 6[7,8] sts at beg of next row and foll alt row. Work 1 row.
Cast off rem 7 sts.
With RS facing rejoin yarn to sts left on spare needle, cast off 15 sts, patt to end.
Complete right side to match left, reversing shapings.

BACK
Work as given for front to **.
Now work straight until back measures same as front to shoulder, ending with a WS row.
Shape shoulders and divide for neck
Next row Cast off 6[7,8] sts, patt 13[14,15] sts including st used to cast off, turn, leaving rem sts on a spare needle and cont on these sts only for right side of neck.
Work 1 row.
Cast off 6[7,8] sts at beg of next row.
Work 1 row.
Cast off rem 7 sts.
With RS facing rejoin yarn to sts on spare needle, cast off 41 sts, patt to end. 19[21,23] sts.
Cast off 6[7,8] sts at beg of next and foll alt row.
Work 1 row. Cast off rem 7 sts.

SLEEVES
Using 4mm (US6) needles, cast on 41[45,49] sts.
Work 8cm (3in) in twisted rib as given for front, ending with a RS row.
Change to 5mm (US8) needles and P 1 row, inc 12 sts evenly across row. 53[57,61] sts.
Cont in mock cable patt as given for 2nd[3rd,1st] size of front, inc 1 st at each end of 13 foll 6th rows. 79[83,87] sts.
Work straight until sleeve measures 40[41,42]cm (16[16¼,16½]in) from top of rib, ending with a WS row.
Shape top
Cast off 5 sts at beg of next 2 rows, then 3 sts at beg of foll 4 rows. Work 1 row. Now (dec 1 st at each end of next row, work 1 row, cast off 2 sts at beg of next 2 rows) 5 times, then cast off 3 sts at beg of next 4 rows. 15[19,23] sts.
Work 1 row.
Cast off.

MAKING UP
Join left shoulder seam.
Neckband
Using 4mm (US6) needles, with RS facing, K up 37 sts evenly across back neck and 44 sts around front neck. 81 sts.
Work 3cm (1¼in) in twisted rib as given for front, ending with a RS row.
K 1 row for foldline. Cont in twisted rib for 3cm (1¼in).
Cast off loosely in rib.
Join right shoulder seam. Fold neckband on to WS and catch down.
Join side and sleeve seams.
Set in sleeves.

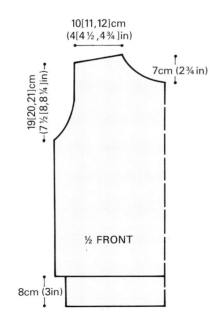

10[11,12]cm (4[4½,4¾]in)
7cm (2¾in)
19[20,21]cm (7½[8,8¼]in)
½ FRONT
8cm (3in)

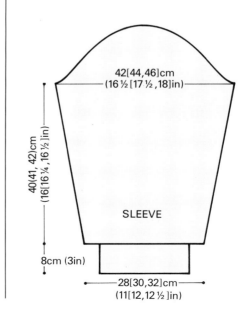

22cm (8¾in)
34[35,36]cm (13½[13¾,14]in)
½ BACK
54[56,58]cm (21¼[22,23]in)

42[44,46]cm (16½[17½,18]in)
40(41,42)cm (16[16¼,16½]in)
SLEEVE
8cm (3in)
28[30,32]cm (11[12,12½]in)

Designed by Valérie Ribadeau Dumas Photograph: Denis Boussard

Pastel Peach

The trellis pattern on this classic round-necked sweater is picked out in purl stitches worked on right-side rows. Made here in soft cotton, it would look equally good in any other plain, smooth yarn.

SIZE
To fit up to 91cm (36in) bust

MATERIALS
700g (25oz) double knitting yarn
1 pair each 3mm (US3) and 4½mm (US7) needles

TENSION
18 sts and 26 rows to 10cm (4in) over patt on 4½mm (US7) needles.

FRONT
Using 3mm (US3) needles, cast on 85 sts.
Work 5cm (2in) K1, P1 rib, inc 15 sts evenly across last row. 100 sts.
Change to 4½mm (US7) needles and commence chart patt as foll (only RS rows shown on chart):
1st row (RS) *K1, P1, K7, P1; rep from *.
2nd row K the P sts of previous row and P the K sts.
3rd row *P1, K1, P1, K5, P1, K1; rep from * to end.
4th row As 2nd row.
These 4 rows set the position of chart patt. Cont in patt, work 5th–20th rows, then rep 1st–20th rows until front measures 28cm (11in) from top of rib, ending with a WS row.
Shape armholes
Cast off 2 sts at beg of next 2 rows, then dec 1 st at each end of next and 5 foll alt rows. 84 sts.**
Work straight until front measures 13cm (5in) from beg of armhole shaping, ending with a RS row.
Divide for neck
Next row Patt 38 sts, turn, leaving rem sts on a spare needle and cont on these sts only for left side of neck.
Cast off 4 sts at beg of next row, 3 sts at beg of foll alt row, then 2 sts at beg of 3 foll alt rows. 25 sts. Now dec 1 st at neck edge on 2 foll alt rows. 23 sts.
Work straight until work measures 21cm (8¼in) from beg of armhole shaping, ending at armhole edge.
Shape shoulder
Cast off.
With RS facing, rejoin yarn to sts on spare needle, cast off 8 sts, patt to end. 38 sts. Complete right side to match left reversing shapings.

BACK
Work as given for front to **.
Now work straight until back measures 19cm (7½in) from beg of armhole shaping, ending with a WS row.
Divide for neck
Next row Patt 31 sts, turn, leaving rem sts on a spare needle and cont on these sts only for right side of neck.

Cast off 8 sts at beg of next row.
Now work straight until back measures 21cm (8½in) from beg of armhole shaping, ending at armhole edge.
Shape shoulder
Cast off.
With RS facing rejoin yarn to sts on spare needle, cast off 22 sts, patt to end. 31 sts. Complete to match right side reversing shapings.

SLEEVES
Using 3mm (US3) needles, cast on 42 sts.
Work 5cm (2in) K1, P1 rib, inc 8 sts evenly across last row. 50 sts.
Change to 4½mm (US7) needles and cont in chart patt as given for front, *at the same time* inc 1 st at each end of next and 8 foll 6th rows, then 1 st at each end of 6 foll 8th rows. 80 sts.
Work straight until sleeve measures 41cm (16in) from top of rib, ending with a WS row.
Shape top
Dec 1 st at each end of next and 5 foll alt rows. 68 sts.
Work straight until sleeve measures 47cm (18½in) from top of rib. Cast off.

MAKING UP
Join right shoulder seam.
Neckband
Using 4½mm (US7) needles, with RS facing K up 90 sts around neck edge.
Work 2.5cm (1in) K1, P1 rib, ending with a WS row. P 1 row for foldline.
Change to 3mm (US3) needles and cont in K1, P1 rib for 2.5cm (1in).
Cast off loosely in rib.
Join left shoulder and neckband seam.
Fold neckband on to WS along foldline and catch down.
Join side and sleeve seams.
Set in sleeves.

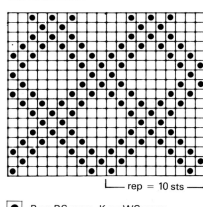

L— rep = 10 sts —J

⬤ P on RS rows, K on WS rows

☐ K on RS rows, P on WS rows

Note RS rows only are shown on chart.

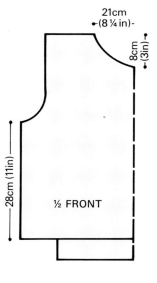

21cm (8¼ in)
8cm (3in)
28cm (11in)
½ FRONT

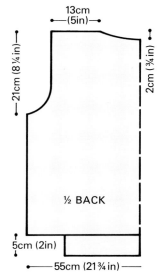

13cm (5in)
21cm (8¼ in)
2cm (¾ in)
½ BACK
5cm (2in)
55cm (21¾ in)

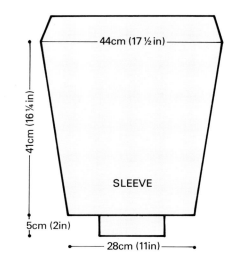

44cm (17½ in)
41cm (16¼ in)
SLEEVE
5cm (2in)
28cm (11in)

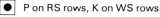

Designed by Valérie Ribadeau Dumas Photograph: Marc Hispard

Basketweave Jacket

A beautifully shaped wrap-around jacket knitted in fine yarn in basketweave pattern. Wear it either belted, as here, or hanging loose over a shirt or sweater.

SIZES
To fit 81[86,91]cm (32[34,36]in) bust

MATERIALS
750[800,850]g 27[29,30]oz four-ply yarn
1 pair 2¾mm (US2) needles

TENSION
33 sts and 44 rows to 10cm (4in) over basketweave patt on 2¾mm (US2) needles.

RIGHT FRONT
Cast on 101[106,111] sts.
Work 2cm (¾in) g st.
Now commence basketweave patt:
1st row (RS) (K5, P5) to last 1[6,1] sts, K1[6,1].
2nd row K1, P0[5,0], (K5, P5) to end.
3rd and 5th rows As 1st row.
4th and 6th rows As 2nd row.
7th, 9th and 11th rows P5, (K5, P5) to last 6[1,6] sts, K6[1,6].
8th, 10th and 12th rows K1[6,1], (P5, K5) to end.
These 12 rows form the patt rep.
Cont in basketweave patt until work measures 34[35,36]cm (13½[13¾,14]in) from top of g st, ending with a RS row.
Shape armhole
Cast off 4 sts at beg of next row, 3 sts at beg of foll alt row and 2 sts at beg of next alt row. 92[97,102] sts.
Work 1 row.
Now dec 1 st at beg of next and foll 4 alt rows. 87[92,97] sts.
Work straight until front measures 13[14,15]cm (5[5½,6]in) from beg of armhole shaping, ending at neck edge.
Shape neck
Cast off 2 sts at beg of next and 17 foll alt rows, then 1 st at beg of 13 foll alt rows, ending at armhole edge.
Shape shoulder
Cast off 9[11,12] sts at beg of next and foll alt row. Work 1 row.
Cast off 10[11,12] sts at beg of next row. Work 1 row.
Cast off rem 10[10,12] sts.

LEFT FRONT
Work as given for right front reversing basketweave patt and all shapings.

BACK
Cast on 167[177,187] sts.
Work 2cm (¾in) g st.
Now work in basketweave patt as foll:
1st row (RS) K1, (K5, P5) to last 6 sts, K6.
2nd row K1, (P5, K5) to last 6 sts, P5, K1.
3rd and 5th rows As 1st row.
4th and 6th rows As 2nd row.

7th, 9th and 11th rows As 2nd row.
8th, 10th and 12th rows As 1st row.
These 12 rows form the patt rep.
Cont in basketweave patt until work measures same as front to armhole, ending with a WS row.
Shape armholes
Cast off 4 sts at beg of next 2 rows, 3 sts at beg of foll 2 rows and 2 sts at beg of foll 2 rows. Now dec 1 st at each end of 5 foll alt rows. 139[149,159] sts.
Work straight until back measures same as front to shoulder, ending with a WS row.
Shape shoulder and divide for neck
Next row Cast off 9[11,12] sts, patt 39[42,46] sts, turn, leaving rem sts on a spare needle and cont on these sts only for first side of neck.
Cast off 10[11,11] sts at beg of next row and 10[11,12] sts at beg of foll row, then 9[10,11] sts at beg of next row.
Cast off rem 10[10,12] sts.
With RS facing rejoin yarn to sts on spare needle, cast off 43 sts, patt to end. 48[53,58] sts.
Next row Cast off 9[11,12] sts, patt to end.
Complete to match first side of neck reversing shapings.

SLEEVES
Cast on 104[110,116] sts.
Work 2cm (¾in) g st.
Commence basketweave patt as foll:
1st row (RS) K2[5,3], (P5, K5) to last 2[5,3] sts, P to end.
2nd row K2[5,3], (P5, K5) to last 2[5,3] sts, P to end.

These 2 rows set the position of the basketweave patt. Cont in patt as for back, *at the same time* inc 1 st at each end of every foll 6th row until there are 132[138,144] sts.
Now work straight until sleeve measures 24[25,26]cm (9½[9¾,10]in) from top of g st border, ending with a WS row.
Shape top
Cast off 3 sts at beg of next 2 rows, then 2 sts at beg of foll 4 rows. Work 1 row. Now dec 1 st at each end of next and every alt row until 32[34,36] sts rem.
Cast off.

POCKETS (make 2)
Cast on 59 sts.
Work 13cm in basketweave patt as given for 1st size of sleeve, then work 2cm (¾in) in g st.
Cast off.

FRONT BORDERS
Cast on 242[250,258] sts.
Work 4cm (1½in) g st.
Cast off.

MAKING UP
Join shoulder seams.
Join side and sleeve seams.
Set in sleeves.
Sew on pockets above g st border, matching basketweave patt and 4cm (1½in) in from front edges.
Join front borders and sew them around back neck and front edges, placing join at centre back neck. Fold borders in half and catch down.

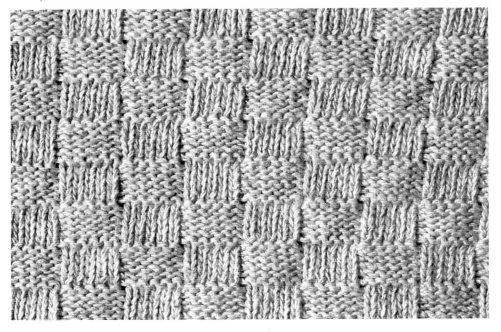

Designed by Christa Fiedler Photograph: Sepp

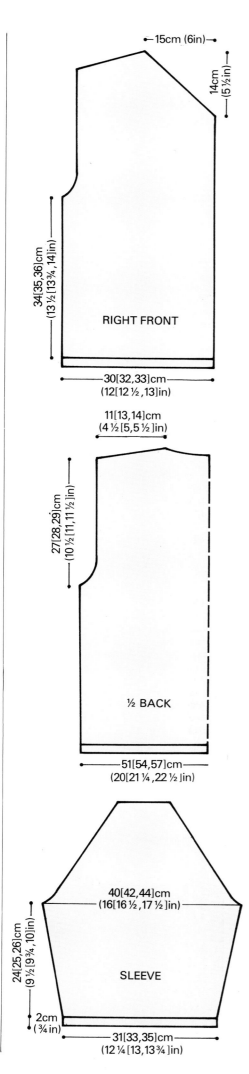

←15cm (6in)→

14cm
(5½in)

34[35,36]cm
(13½[13¾,14]in)

RIGHT FRONT

30[32,33]cm
(12[12½,13]in)

11[13,14]cm
(4½[5,5½]in)

27[28,29]cm
(10½[11,11½]in)

½ BACK

51[54,57]cm
(20[21¼,22½]in)

40[42,44]cm
(16[16½,17½]in)

24[25,26]cm
(9½[9¾,10]in)

SLEEVE

2cm
(¾in)

31[33,35]cm
(12¼[13,13¾]in)

Paris Blue

Raid the ragbag for the yarn for this loose cardigan. It's worked in stocking stitch in strips of light cotton fabric. The faint-hearted can use extra-chunky yarn instead.

SIZE
To fit up to 91cm (36in) bust

MATERIALS
Approx 8m (9yd) 150cm (60in) wide lightweight fabric
1 pair 7mm (US10½) and 8mm (US11) needles
1 7mm (US10½) circular needle
2 buttons

TENSION
9 sts and 11 rows to 10cm (4in) over st st on 8mm (US11) needles.

SPECIAL NOTE
Wash fabric well to remove dressing, then dry and iron it and cut it into 1cm (½in) wide bias strips. Seam or knot strips together and roll into balls.

POCKET LININGS (make 2)
Using 8mm (US11) needles, cast on 11 sts. Work 14 rows st st, end with a P row. Leave these sts on a spare needle.

RIGHT FRONT
Using 7mm (US10½) needles, cast on 23 sts. Work 5cm (2in) K1, P1 rib. Change to 8mm (US11) needles and work in st st for 14 rows, end with a P row.
Place pocket
Next row K11 sts, sl next 11 sts on to stitch holder, K across 11 pocket lining sts, K to last st, inc 1. 24 sts. Cont in st st, work 3 rows.
Shape front neck
Cont in st st, inc 1 st at side edge on foll 11th row, *at the same time* dec 1 st at neck edge on next and every foll 6th row until work measures 34cm (13½in) from top of rib, ending at side edge.
Shape armhole
Cast off 3 sts at beg of next row, then dec 1 st at armhole edge on 3 foll alt rows, *at the same time* cont to dec at neck edge on every 6th row as set until 12 sts rem. Work straight until front measures 26cm (10in) from beg of armhole shaping, ending at armhole edge.
Shape shoulder
Cast off 6 sts at beg of next row. Work 1 row. Cast off rem 6 sts.

LEFT FRONT
Work as given for right front, reversing pocket placing and all shapings.

BACK
Using 7mm (US10½) needles, cast on 46 sts. Work 5cm (2in) K1, P1 rib. Change to 8mm (US11) needles and cont in st st, inc 1 st at each end of 15th and foll 14th row. 50 sts.

Work straight until back matches front to armhole shaping, end with a WS row.
Shape armholes
Cast off 3 sts at beg of next 2 rows and dec 1 st at each end of next and foll 2 alt rows. 38 sts.
Now work straight until back matches front to shoulder, ending with a WS row.
Shape shoulders and divide for back neck
Next row Cast off 6 sts, K6 including st used to cast off, turn, leaving rem sts on a spare needle and cont on these sts only for first side of neck.
Work 1 row. Cast off rem 6 sts.
With RS of work facing rejoin yarn to sts on spare needle, cast off 14 sts, K to end. 12 sts. Cast off 6 sts at beg of next row.
Work 1 row. Cast off rem 6 sts.

SLEEVES
Using 7mm (US10½) needles, cast on 27 sts. Work 4cm (1½in) K1, P1 rib. Change to 8mm (US11) needles and work in st st, *at the same time* inc 1 st at each end of every foll 4th and 6th rows alt until there are 43 sts.
Work straight until sleeve measures 40cm (16in) from top of rib.
Shape top
Cast off 3 sts at beg of next 2 rows and 2 sts at beg of foll 10 rows, then 3 sts at beg of foll 2 rows. Cast off rem 11 sts.

POCKET EDGINGS
Using 7mm (US10½) needles, with RS of work facing, K across 11 sts left on stitch holder at pocket opening. Work 2cm (¾in) K1, P1 rib. Cast off in rib.

MAKING UP
Catch down pocket linings to WS of fronts. Slipstitch pocket edgings to RS of fronts. Join shoulder seams. Join side and sleeve seams. Set in sleeves.
Front band
Using 7mm (US10½) circular needle, with RS of work facing and beg at lower right front edge, K up 19 sts to beg of neck shaping, 41 sts to shoulder seam, 21 sts across back neck, 41 sts to beg of left front neck shaping and 19 sts to left front lower edge. 141 sts.
Work in K1, P1 rib *at the same time* make buttonholes on 2nd and 3rd rows as foll:
2nd row Rib 5, cast off 2 sts, rib 8 including st used to cast off, cast off 2 sts, rib to end.
3rd row Rib to end casting on 2 sts over those cast off in previous row.
Cont in rib until front band measures 4cm (1½in).
Cast off in rib. Sew on buttons.

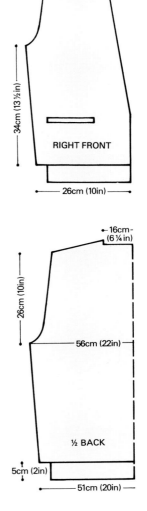

RIGHT FRONT

←13cm (5in)→ ←8cm (3in)→
34cm (13½in)
26cm (10in)

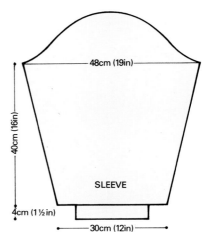

←16cm (6¼in)→
26cm (10in)
56cm (22in)
½ BACK
5cm (2in)
←51cm (20in)→

SLEEVE
48cm (19in)
40cm (16in)
4cm (1½in)
←30cm (12in)→

Designed by Yuki Torii Photograph: Fouli Elia

Cotton Bobbles

This pretty cardigan could be knitted in thick cotton yarn, as here, or something warmer, such as wool or even mohair. The cable and bobbly panels run down the sleeves and fronts but the back is in plain moss stitch.

SPRING
★ ★

SIZES
To fit age 4[6,8] years

MATERIALS
250[300,350]g 9[11,13]oz double knitting yarn
1 pair each 3¾mm (US5) and 4½mm (US7) needles
7 buttons

TENSION
18 sts and 29 rows to 10cm (4in) over moss st on 4½mm (US7) needles.

PANEL PATT
Worked over 13 sts.
1st row (RS) P4, K2, P1, K2, P4.
2nd and every alt row P the K sts and K the P sts of previous row.
3rd row P3, K2 tog, K1, yrn, P1, yon, K1, K2 tog tbl, P3.
5th row P2, K2 tog, K1, yrn, P3, yon, K1, K2 tog tbl, P2.
7th row P1, K2 tog, K1, yrn, P5, yon, K1, K2 tog tbl, P1.
9th row P1, K2, P3, K into front and back of next st twice then lift 1st, 2nd and 3rd sts over 4th st and off needle to make bobble, P3, K2, P1.
11th row P to end.
12th row As 2nd row.
These 12 rows form the panel patt.

RIGHT FRONT
Using 3¾mm (US5) needles, cast on 31[33,35] sts.
Next row (RS) K4, (K1, P1) to last st, K1.
Next row (P1, K1) to last 5 sts, P1, K4.
Rep these 2 rows until work measures 1.5cm (¾in), ending with a WS row.
Make buttonhole
Next row K2, yfwd, K2 tog, (K1, P1) to last st, K1.
Cont in rib and g st border as set until work measures 3cm (1¼in) from cast-on edge, ending with a WS row.
Change to 4½mm (US7) needles and commence patt as foll:
1st row (RS) K4, (K1, P1) 2[3,3] times, K2[1,2], 1st row panel patt, K1, (K1, P1) 3[4,4] times, K1[0,1].
2nd row P0[1,0], (K1, P1) 4[4,5] times, 2nd row panel patt, K 0[1,0], (P1, K1) 3[3,4] times, K4.
These 2 rows set the position of panel patt with moss st and g st buttonhole band.
Cont in patt as set making 3 more buttonholes as before at 4.5[5,5.5]cm (1¾[2,2¼]in) intervals, until work measures 15[17,19]cm (6[6½,7½]in) from the top of the rib, ending at the armhole edge.

Shape armhole
Cast off 2 sts at beg of next row. 29[31, 33] sts.
Now work straight, making 2 more buttonholes at same intervals as before, until front measures 10[11,12]cm (4[4½,4¾]in) from beg of armhole shaping, ending at armhole edge.
Shape neck
Next row Patt to last 4 sts, turn, leaving rem 4 sts on a stitch holder.
Cast off 2 sts at beg of next and foll 2 alt rows, then dec 1 st at beg of next 2 alt rows, ending at armhole edge.
Cast off rem 17[19,21] sts.

LEFT FRONT
Work as given for right front, omitting buttonholes and reversing panel patt and all shapings.

BACK
Using 3¾mm (US5) needles, cast on 55[59,63] sts.
Work 3cm (1¼in) K1, P1 rib.
Change to 4½mm (US7) needles and work in moss st until back measures 15[17,19]cm (6[6½,7½]in) from top of rib, ending with a WS row.
Shape armholes
Cast off 2 sts at beg of next 2 rows. 51 [55,59] sts.
Now work straight until back measures 12[13,14]cm (4¾[5,5½]in) from beg of armhole shaping, ending with a WS row.
Divide for neck
Next row Patt 16[18,20] sts, turn, leaving rem sts on a spare needle and cont on these sts only for first side of neck.
Work straight until back measures same as front to cast-off edge.
Cast off.

With RS of work facing rejoin yarn to sts on spare needle, cast off 19 sts, patt to end.
Complete to match first side of neck.

SLEEVES
Join shoulder seams.
Using 4½mm (US7) needles, with RS of work facing, K up 49[53,57] sts, along armhole edge.
Next row (K1, P1) 9[10,11] times, K4, P2, K1, P2, K4, (P1, K1) 9[10,11] times.
Now commence panel patt as foll:
1st row (RS) (K1, P1) 8[9,10] times, K2, 1st row panel patt, K2, (P1, K1) 8[9,10] times.
2nd row (K1, P1) 9[10,11] times, 2nd row panel patt, (P1, K1) 9[10,11] times.
These 2 rows set position of panel patt and moss st.
Cont as set, dec 1 st at each end of 10th and 3 foll 14th rows. 41[45,49] sts.
Work straight until sleeve measures 20[22,24]cm (8[8½,9½]in).
Change to 3¾mm (US5) needles and work 2cm (¾in) K1, P1 rib.
Cast off in rib.

MAKING UP
Join side and sleeve seams.
Neckband
Using 3¾mm (US5) needles, with RS of work facing K across 4 sts left on right front border, K up 47 sts evenly round neck edge, K across 4 sts left at left front border. 55 sts.
Work 2cm (¾in) K1, P1 rib, making buttonhole on 4th row as foll:
Buttonhole row Rib 2, yfwd, rib 2 tog, rib to end.
Cast off in rib. Sew on buttons.

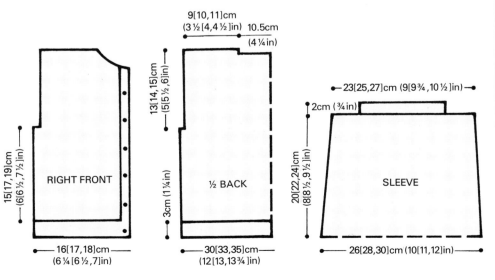

9[10,11]cm (3½[4,4½]in)   10.5cm (4¼in)

13[14,15]cm (5[5½,6]in)

15[17,19]cm (6[6½,7½]in)

3cm (1¼in)

RIGHT FRONT

½ BACK

16[17,18]cm (6¼[6½,7]in)

30[33,35]cm (12[13,13¾]in)

23[25,27]cm (9[9¾,10½]in)

2cm (¾in)

20[22,24]cm (8[8½,9½]in)

SLEEVE

26[28,30]cm (10[11,12]in)

Designed by Soyzic Cornu Photograph: François Pomepui

Half-Mast

This wide-bodied, boxy sweater is patterned in crisp houndstooth checks. Knitted here in soft acrylic yarn, it would also work beautifully in a smooth cotton or a fine bouclé.

SPRING
★ ★

SIZES
To fit 81[86,91]cm (32[34,36]in) bust

MATERIALS
250[300,350]g (9[11,13]oz) four-ply yarn in main colour (A)
100g (4oz) four-ply yarn in contrast colour (B)
1 pair each 2¼mm (US1) and 3mm (US3) needles

TENSION
30 sts and 39 rows to 10cm (4in) over patt on 3mm (US3) needles.

FRONT
Using 2¼mm (US1) needles and A, cast on 144[152,160] sts.
Work 3cm (1¼in) K1, P1 rib, inc 8 sts evenly across last row. 152[160,168] sts.
Change to 3mm (US3) needles and work 2 rows in st st, beg with a K row.
Commence chart patt, work in st st throughout, as foll:
1st row (RS) *K1A, 1B, 1A, 3B, 1A, 1B; rep from * to end.
2nd row *P1B, 5A, 1B, 1A; rep from * to end.
These 2 rows set the position of the chart patt.
****Cont in patt as set, work 1st–18th rows once, then rep 11th–18th rows throughout until front measures 35[37,39]cm (13¾[14½,15½]in) from top of rib, ending with a WS row.
Divide for neck
Next row Patt 66[70,74] sts, turn, leaving rem sts on a spare needle and cont on these sts only for left side of neck.
Cast off 2 sts at beg of next and foll alt

row, then dec 1 st at neck edge on foll 8[11,12] alt rows. 52[55,58] sts.
Work 8[2,0] rows straight, thus ending at armhole edge.
Shape shoulder
Cast off 13 sts at beg of next row and then cast off 13[14,15] sts at beg of foll 2 alt rows.
Work 1 row.
Cast off rem 13[14,15] sts.
With RS facing rejoin yarn to sts on spare needle, cast off 20 sts, patt to end. 66[70,74] sts.
Complete to match left side reversing shapings.

BACK
Work as given for front to **.
Cont in patt as set until back measures same as front to shoulder, ending at armhole edge.
Shape shoulder and divide for neck
Next row Cast off 13 sts, patt 49[53,57] sts, turn, leaving rem sts on a spare needle and cont on these sts only for right side of neck.
Cast off 2[3,4] sts at beg of next row and 4 sts at beg of 2 foll alt rows, *at the same time* cast off for shoulder 13[14,15] sts at beg of next 2 alt rows.
Cast off rem 13[14,15] sts.
With RS of work facing, rejoin yarn to sts on spare needle, cast off 28 sts, patt to end of row.
Work 1 row.
Complete to match right side, reversing shapings.

SLEEVES
Using 2¼mm (US1) needles and A, cast on 104[112,120] sts.

Work 3cm (1¼in) K1, P1 rib.
Change to 3mm (US3) needles and work 2 rows st st.
Now work in patt from chart as for front, *at the same time* inc 1 st at each end of every alt row until there are 150[156,162] sts.
Work straight until sleeve measures 16[17,18]cm (6¼[6½,7]in) from top of rib.
Cast off.

MAKING UP
Join right shoulder seam.
Neckband
Using 2¼mm (US1) needles and A, with RS facing K up 148 sts evenly around neck edge.
Work 2cm (¾in) K1, P1 rib.
Cast off in rib.
Join left shoulder seam.
Set sleeves in flat, matching the centre of the cast-off edge of the sleeve to the shoulder seam.
Join side and sleeve seams.

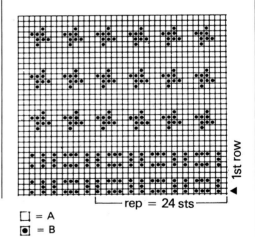

◀ 1st row

rep = 24 sts

□ = A
⦿ = B

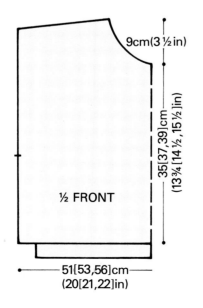

9cm(3½in)

35[37,39]cm (13¾[14½,15½]in)

½ FRONT

51[53,56]cm (20[21,22]in)

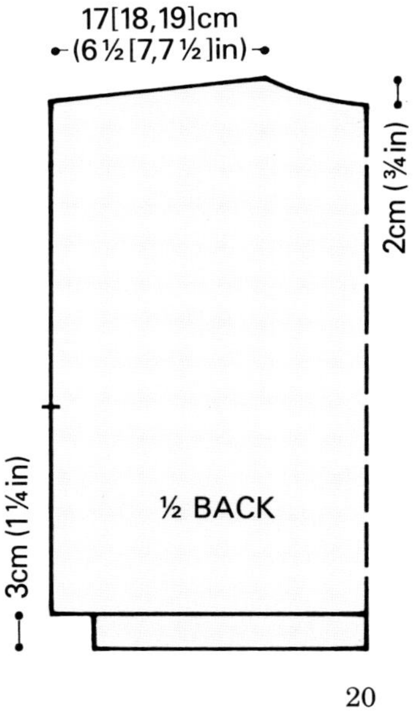

17[18,19]cm (6½[7,7½]in)

2cm (¾in)

½ BACK

3cm (1¼in)

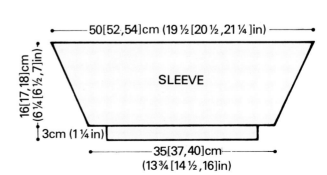

50[52,54]cm (19½[20½,21¼]in)

16[17,18]cm (6¼[6½,7]in)

SLEEVE

3cm (1¼in)

35[37,40]cm (13¾[14½,16]in)

Designed by Fac Bazaar Photograph: Sepp

Deauville

Striped in three cool colours, a long-sleeved sweater with a nautical flavour, knitted in medium-weight cotton.

SIZE
To fit 81–91cm (32–36in) bust

MATERIALS
350g (13oz) double knitting yarn in main colour (A)
200g (8oz) double knitting yarn in 1st contrast colour (B)
100g (4oz) double knitting yarn in 2nd contrast colour (C)
1 pair each 3¼mm (US4) and 4½mm (US7) needles

TENSION
19 sts and 28 rows to 10cm (4in) over st st on 4½mm (US7) needles.

FRONT
Using 3¼mm (US4) needles and A, cast on 98 sts.
Work 4 rows K2, P2 rib.
Change to 4½mm (US7) needles and work in st st in stripes as foll: 12 rows in A, 14 rows in B, 14 rows in A, 14 rows in C, (14 rows in A, 14 rows in B) twice, *at the same time*, when work measures 24cm (9½in) ending with a WS row, shape armholes as foll: cast off 4 sts at beg of next 2 rows, then 2 sts at beg of foll 2 rows; now dec 1 st at each end of next row. 84 sts.
Keeping the stripe sequence correct (and changing to yarn A when the third stripe in yarn B is completed), work straight until the front of the sweater measures 19cm (7½in) from the beg of armhole shaping, ending with a WS row.*

Divide for neck
Next row K37, turn, leaving rem sts on a spare needle, cont on these sts only for left side of neck.
**Cast off 5 sts at beg of next row, 4 sts at beg of foll alt row, 2 sts at beg of foll 2 alt rows and 1 st at beg of next alt row. 23 sts.
Work 4 rows straight, thus ending at armhole edge.
Shape shoulder
Cast off.
Return to sts on spare needle, with RS facing cast off 10 sts, cont in patt to end of row. Work 1 row.
Complete right side of neck to match left side of neck, working as set from** to end.

BACK
Work as given for front to *. Now work straight until back measures 22cm (8½in) from beg of armhole shaping, ending with a WS row.
Divide for neck
Next row K28, turn, leaving rem sts on a spare needle and cont on these sts only for right side of neck.
***Cast off 5 sts at beg of next row. 23 sts.
Work straight until back matches front to beg of shoulder shaping, ending at armhole edge.
Shape shoulder
Cast off.
Return to sts on spare needle, with RS facing cast off 28 sts, patt to end of row. Work 1 row.

Complete left side of neck to match right side of neck, working as set from *** to end.

SLEEVES
Using 3¼mm (US4) needles and A, cast on 58 sts.
Work 4 rows K2, P2 rib.
Change to 4½mm (US7) needles and work in st st inc 1 st at each end of every 6th row until there are 88 sts, *at the same time* cont in stripe sequence as foll: 12 rows in A, (14 rows in B, 14 rows in A) twice, 14 rows in C, 14 rows in A, 14 rows in B (changing to A when third 14-row stripe in B is completed) cont to inc as set until sleeve measures 35cm (13¾in) from cast-on edge, ending with a WS row.
Shape top
Cast off 4 sts at beg of next 2 rows, and 2 sts at beg of foll 4 rows. Now dec 1 st at each end of foll 11 alt rows, then cast off 2 sts at beg of foll 2 rows and 4 sts at beg of next 2 rows. 38 sts.
Cast off.

MAKING UP
Join right shoulder seam.
Neckband
Using 3¼mm (US4) needles and A, with RS of work facing K up 84 sts evenly around neck edge.
Work 3 rows K2, P2 rib.
Cast off in rib.
Join left shoulder seam and side seams.
Join sleeve seams.
Set in sleeves.

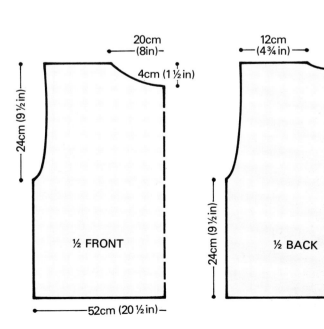

20cm (8in)
4cm (1½in)
24cm (9½in)
½ FRONT
52cm (20½in)

12cm (4¾in)
24cm (9½in)
½ BACK

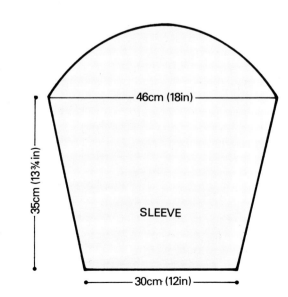

46cm (18in)
35cm (13¾in)
SLEEVE
30cm (12in)

Designed by Valérie Ribadeau Dumas Photograph: François Pomepui

Cabled Pullover

A great garment for active youngsters, this V-neck pullover has two different cables and contrasting striped welts. Alternatively, make it in one colour only.

SIZE
To fit age 6 years

MATERIALS
150g (6oz) double knitting yarn in main colour (A)
50g (2oz) in contrast colour (B)
1 pair each 4mm (US6) and 5mm (US8) needles

TENSION
30 sts and 26 rows to 10cm (4in) on 5mm (US8) needles, over patt as foll:
1st row P2, Tw2L twice, P2, K6, P2, Tw2L twice, P2, K6, P2.
2nd row P the K sts and K the P sts of previous row.
3rd row P2, Tw2R twice, P2, C6B, P2, Tw2R twice, P2, C6B, P2.
4th row As 2nd row.
Rep these 4 rows 5 times more then the first 2 rows again.

SPECIAL ABBREVIATIONS
Tw2R (twist 2 right)—K into front of 2nd st on LH needle, then into front of 1st st, dropping both sts off needle at the same time.
Tw2L (twist 2 left)—K tbl 2nd st on LH needle then K into front of 1st st, dropping both sts off needle at the same time.
C6B (cable 6 back)—sl next 3 sts on to cable needle and hold at back of work, K3, then K3 from cable needle.

FRONT
Using 4mm (US6) needles and B, cast on 92 sts.
Work in K1, P1 rib as foll:
3 rows in B, 2 rows in A, (2 rows in B, 2 rows in A) twice, 3 rows in B, 1 row in A, inc 10 sts evenly across last row. 102 sts.
Change to 5mm (US8) needles and cont in A, commence patt as foll:
1st row (RS) P2, Tw2L twice, *P2, K6, P2, Tw2L twice, P2, Tw2L twice; rep from * to last 16 sts, P2, K6, P2, Tw2L twice, P2.
2nd and every alt row P the K sts and K the P sts of previous row.
3rd row P2, Tw2R twice, *P2, C6B, P2, Tw2R twice, P2, Tw2R twice; rep from * to last 16 sts, P2, C6B, P2, Tw2R twice, P2.
4th row As 2nd row.
Rep 1st–4th rows.
Cont in patt until front measures 22cm (8½in), ending with a WS row.**
Shape armholes and divide for neck
Next row Cast off 5 sts, patt 44 sts, K2 tog, turn, leaving rem sts on a spare needle and cont on these sts only for left side of neck. 45 sts.

Work 1 row. Cast off 4 sts at beg of next row and 3 sts at beg of 2 foll alt rows, *at the same time* dec 1 st at neck edge on next and every alt row until 15 sts rem. Work 3 rows straight, thus ending at armhole edge.
Shape shoulder
Cast off 5 sts at beg of next and foll alt row.
Work 1 row.
Cast off.
With RS facing rejoin yarn to sts on spare needle, K2 tog, patt to end.
Next row Cast off 5, patt to end. 45 sts.
Complete right side to match left reversing shapings.

BACK
Work as given for front to **.
Shape armholes
Cast off 5 sts at beg of next 2 rows, 4 sts at beg of foll 2 rows and 3 sts at beg of foll 4 rows. 72 sts.
Now work straight until back measures same as front to shoulder shaping, ending with a WS row.
Shape shoulders and divide for neck
Next row Cast off 5 sts, patt 15 sts, turn, leaving rem sts on a spare needle and cont on these sts only for right side of back.
Cast off 5 sts at beg of next 2 rows.

Work 1 row. Cast off rem 5 sts.
With RS facing rejoin yarn to sts on spare needle, cast off 32 sts, patt to end. 20 sts.
Cast off 5 sts at beg of next 3 rows.
Work 1 row.
Cast off rem 5 sts.

MAKING UP
Join right shoulder seam.
Neckband
Using 4mm (US6) needles and B, with RS facing K 48 sts down left side of neck, 48 sts up right side of neck and 36 sts across back neck. 132 sts.
Work in K1, P1 rib as foll: 2 rows in B, 2 rows in A, 2 rows in B, *at the same time* dec at front neck on each row as foll:
RS rows Rib to within 2 sts of point of V, sl 1, K1, psso, K2 tog, rib to end.
WS rows Rib to within 2 sts of point of V, P2 tog, P2 tog tbl, rib to end.
Cast off in rib, dec as before.
Join left shoulder seam.
Armbands
Using 4mm (US6) needles and B, with RS facing, K up 88 sts around armhole edge.
Work in K1, P1 rib in colour sequence as given for neckband.
Cast off in rib.
Join side seams.

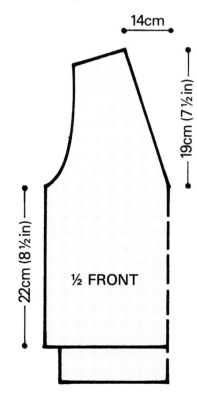

14cm
19cm (7½in)
22cm (8½in)
½ FRONT

5cm (2in)
17cm (6½in)
2cm (¾in)
½ BACK
34cm (13½in)

Designed by Valérie Ribadeau Dumas Photograph: François Pomepui

In the Pink

This broad-ribbed sweater could certainly be made in a weekend. Try substituting a flecked or textured yarn for this plain smooth wool.

SIZE
To fit 81–91cm (32–36in) bust

MATERIALS
450g (16oz) Aran-weight yarn
1 pair each 4mm (US6) and 4½mm (US7) needles

TENSION
21 sts and 26 rows to 10cm (4in) over K3, P3 rib on 4½mm (US7) needles using yarn singly.

FRONT
Using 4mm (US6) needles and yarn double, cast on 91 sts.
K 2 rows.
Change to single yarn.
Next row K to end, inc 16 sts evenly across row. 107 sts.
Change to 4½mm (US7) needles and work in K3, P3 rib as foll:
1st row (RS) K1, P3, *K3, P3; rep from * to last st, K1.
2nd row K1, *K3, P3; rep from * to last 4 sts, K4.
These 2 rows form the patt rep.
Cont in K3, P3 rib until work measures 23cm (9in) from cast-on edge, ending with a WS row.
Shape armholes
Cast off 3 sts at beg of next 2 rows, then dec 1 st at each end of next and foll alt row. 97 sts.**
Now work straight until front measures 43cm (17in) from cast-on edge, ending with a WS row.

Divide for neck
Next row Patt 42 sts, turn, leaving rem sts on a spare needle and cont on these sts only for left side of neck.
***Cast off 5 sts at beg of next row, 4 sts at beg of foll alt row, 3 sts at beg of next alt row and 2 sts at beg of foll alt row.
Dec 1 st at beg of next alt row. 27 sts.
Work straight until armhole measures 23cm (9in), ending at armhole edge.
Shape shoulder
Cast off 9 sts at beg of next and foll alt row. Work 1 row.
Cast off rem 9 sts.
With RS facing rejoin yarn to sts on spare needle, cast off 13 sts, patt to end.
Work 1 row.
Complete right side to match left working from *** to end.

BACK
Work as given for front to **.
Now work straight until back measures 23cm (9in) from beg of armhole shaping, ending with a WS row.
Shape shoulders and divide for back neck
Next row Cast off 9 sts, patt 18 sts, turn, leaving rem sts on a spare needle and cont on these sts only for right side of neck. 18 sts.
Work 1 row.
****Cast off 9 sts at beg of next row.
Work 1 row.
Cast off rem 9 sts.
With RS facing rejoin yarn to sts on spare needle, cast off 43 sts, patt to end.

Cast off 9 sts at beg of next and foll alt row.
Work 1 row.
Cast off rem 9 sts.

SLEEVES
Using 4mm (US6) needles and yarn double cast on 63 sts.
K 2 rows.
Change to single yarn.
Next row K to end, inc 8 sts evenly across row. 71 sts.
Change to 4½mm (US7) needles.
Work in K3, P3 rib as given for front, inc 1 st at each end of 12 foll 8th rows. 95 sts.
Work straight until sleeve measures 40cm (16in) from cast-on edge, ending with a WS row.
Shape top
Cast off 4 sts at beg of next 2 rows and 3 sts at beg of foll 8 rows. 63 sts.
Work 1 row.
Cast off.

MAKING UP
Join right shoulder seam.
Neckband
Using 4mm (US6) needles and yarn double, with RS facing, K up 91 sts evenly around neck edge.
K 2 rows.
Cast off as foll:
Cast-off row (Cast off 3 sts, cast off 2 tog) to last st, cast off.
Join left shoulder seam.
Join side and sleeve seams.
Set in sleeves.

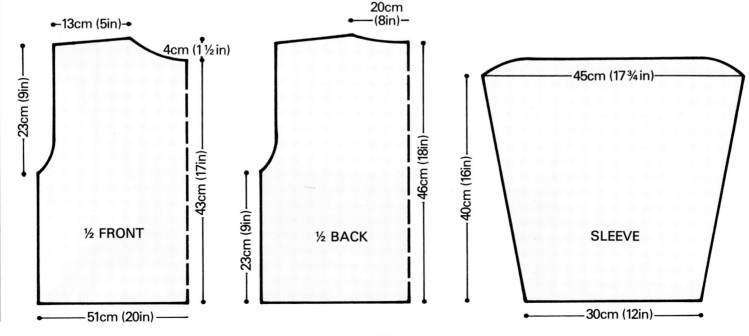

Designed by Valérie Ribadeau Dumas Photograph: François Pomepui

Breton

The twists and turns of this trellis pattern are made without using a cable needle, so it's a lot easier to make than might be expected. Knitted here in a mixed cotton, viscose and linen yarn with a slub finish, it would look just as stylish in wool.

SPRING
★ ★

SIZE
To fit up to 96cm (38in) bust

MATERIALS
700g (25oz) Aran-weight yarn
1 pair each 4mm (US6), 4½mm (US7) and 5mm (US8) needles

TENSION
17 sts and 18 rows to 10cm (4in) over K2, P3 rib on 5mm (US8) needles.

SPECIAL ABBREVIATIONS
Tw2L (twist 2 left)—pass RH needle behind 1st st on LH needle and P 2nd st, then K 1st st, dropping both sts off RH needle at the same time.
Tw2R (twist 2 right)—pass RH needle in front of 1st st on LH needle and K 2nd st, then P 1st st, dropping both sts off RH needle at the same time.
C2 (cable 2)—pass RH needle behind 1st st on LH needle and K 2nd st, then K 1st st, dropping both sts off RH needle at the same time.

CABLE PATT SEQUENCE
1st row (RS) P1, *K1, P2, K1, P1; rep from * to end.
2nd, 4th and 6th rows K the P sts and P the K sts of previous row.
3rd row P1, *Tw2L, Tw2R, P1; rep from * to end.
5th row P1, *P1, C2, P2; rep from * to end.
7th row P1, *Tw2R, Tw2L, P1; rep from * to end.
8th row K to end.
These 8 rows form cable patt.
Now work 23 rows K2, P3 rib, ending with a RS row.
K 1 row.
Rep 1st–8th rows of cable patt 3 times.
Work 23 rows K2, P3 rib, ending with a RS row.
K 1 row.
Work 1st–8th rows cable patt.
These 88 rows form the cable patt sequence.

FRONT
Using 4½mm (US7) needles, cast on 77 sts. Work in K2, P3 rib as foll:
1st row (RS) *K2, P3; rep from * to last 2 sts, K2.
2nd row *P2, K3; rep from * to last 2 sts, P2.
Rep these 2 rows.
Cont in rib until work measures 4cm (1½in), ending with a WS row.
Next row K to end, inc 9 sts evenly across row. 86 sts.
Next row K to end.
Change to 5mm (US8) needles and commence cable patt sequence.
Cont in patt until work measures 22cm (8½in) from inc row, end with a WS row.
Shape armholes
Keeping patt correct, cast off 4 sts at beg of next 2 rows, then dec 1 st at each end of next and 2 foll alt rows. 72 sts.**
Cont in patt until work measures 17cm (6½in) from beg of armhole shaping, ending with a WS row.
Divide for neck
Next row Patt 31 sts, turn, leaving rem sts on a spare needle and cont on these sts only for first side of neck.
Cast off 4 sts at beg of next row and 3 sts at beg of foll alt row, then 2 sts at beg of next 2 alt rows. Work 3 rows.
Now dec 1 st at neck edge on next and foll 4th row. 18 sts.
Cont in patt until cable patt sequence is complete. Cast off.
With RS facing rejoin yarn to sts on spare needle, cast off 10 sts, patt to end.
Complete to match first side reversing shaping.

BACK
Work as given for front to **.
Now cont in patt as given for front, omitting neck shaping, until back matches front to shoulder. Cast off.

SLEEVES
Using 4½mm (US7) needles, cast on 42 sts. Work in K2, P3 rib as given for front for 4cm (1½in), ending with a WS row.
Next row K to end, inc 9 sts evenly across last row. 51 sts.
Next row K to end.
Change to 5mm (US8) needles and work 8 rows in cable patt as given for front, inc 1 st at each end of 6th row. 53 sts.
Now cont in K2, P3 rib, inc 1 st at each end of alt 4th and 5th rows until there are 77 sts. Work straight until sleeve measures 39cm (15in) from inc row, ending with a WS row.
Shape top
Now work 8 rows cable patt, *at the same time* cast off 4 sts at beg of next 2 rows, then dec 1 st at each end of next and 2 foll alt rows. Cast off rem 63 sts.

MAKING UP
Join right shoulder seam.
Neckband
Using 4mm (US6) needles, with RS of work facing, K up 87 sts evenly around neck edge.
Work 2.5cm (1in) K2, P3 rib.
Cast off in rib.
Join left shoulder and neckband seam.
Join side and sleeve seams.
Set in sleeves.

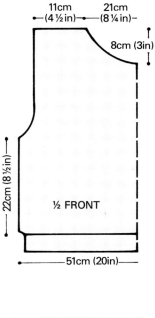

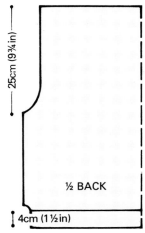

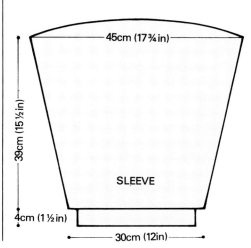

Designed by Valérie Ribadeau Dumas Photograph: Gérard Mareschal

Mini-Dress

Stay cool in a skimpy sun-dress worked in a slipstitch pattern in a fine mercerised cotton yarn.

SIZE
To fit 81–91cm (32–36in) bust

MATERIALS
350g (13oz) double knitting yarn
1 pair each 3mm (US3) and 4mm (US6) needles
1 set four double-pointed 3mm (US3) needles

TENSION
21 sts and 34 rows to 10cm (4in) over patt on 4mm (US6) needles.

SPECIAL NOTE
Do not count extra sts, made as part of patt, when making st checks after incs or decs.

FRONT
Using 3mm (US3) needles, cast on 113 sts.
Work 4 rows g st.
Change to 4mm (US6) needles and cont in slipstitch patt:
1st row (WS) K1, *yfwd, sl 1 P-wise, K1; rep from * to end.
2nd row K1, *K tog tbl sl st and yfwd of previous row, K1; rep from * to end.
These 2 rows form the patt rep.
Cont in patt until work measures 18cm (7in) from cast-on edge.
Work 1 row in slipstitch patt, dec 1 st at each end. 111 sts.
Cont in patt until work measures 32cm (12½in) from cast-on edge.
Work 1 row in slipstitch patt, dec 1 st at each end. 109 sts.
Now work straight until work measures 51cm (20in) from cast-on edge, ending with a WS row.
Shape armholes
Cast off 5 sts at beg of next 2 rows, then 4 sts at beg of foll 2 rows and 3 sts at beg of next 2 rows. 85 sts.
Now cast off 2 sts at beg of next 2 rows, then dec 1 st at each end of next row. 79 sts.**
Work 7 rows straight, thus ending with a WS row.
Divide for neck
Next row Patt 31 sts, turn, leaving rem sts on a spare needle and cont on these sts only for first side of neck.
Cast off 4 sts at beg of next row and 3 sts at beg of foll 2 alt rows, then 2 sts at beg of next alt row. 19 sts.
Work 1 row.
Now dec 1 st at neck edge on next and foll 5 alt rows, *at the same time* dec 1 st at armhole edge on next and 2 foll 14th rows. 10 sts.
Work straight until front measures 27cm (10½in) from beg of armhole

shaping.
Cast off.
With RS facing rejoin yarn to sts on spare needle, cast off 17 sts, patt to end. 31 sts.
Complete second side of front neck to match first side of front neck, reversing shapings.

BACK
Work as given for front to **.
Patt 14 rows, dec 1 st at each end of last row. 77 sts.
Divide for neck
Next row Patt 27 sts, turn, leaving rem sts on a spare needle and cont on these sts only for first side of neck.
Cast off 4 sts at beg of next row, 3 sts at beg of foll alt row and 2 sts at beg of next alt row. 18 sts.
Work 1 row.
Now dec 1 st at neck edge on next and 5 foll alt rows, *at the same time* dec 1 st at armhole edge on 7th and foll 14th row. 10 sts.

Work straight until back matches front to cast-off edge.
Cast off.
With WS facing rejoin yarn to sts on spare needle, cast off 23 sts, cont in patt to end.
Complete second side of neck to match first side, reversing shapings.

MAKING UP
Join shoulder seams very neatly.
Armhole edgings
With RS of work facing, using 3mm (US3) needles, K up 136 sts evenly around armhole edge.
Work 3 rows g st.
Cast off.
Neckband
With RS of work facing, using double-pointed 3mm (US3) needles, beg at left shoulder seam K up 120 sts evenly around front neck and 100 sts evenly around back neck. 220 sts.
Work 3 rounds g st.
Cast off.

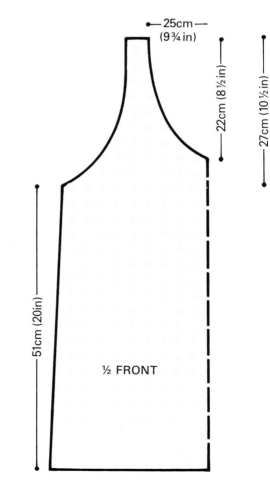

Designed by Valérie Ribadeau Dumas   Photograph: Mike Yavel

Sloppy Joe

A wonderfully loose cool sweater with a deep V-neck at front and back. Knitted here in a fine yarn mixture of cotton and viscose but the simple shape would suit many fibres and textures—silk would be stunning.

SIZES
To fit 81–86[91–96]cm (32–34 [36–38]in) bust

MATERIALS
500[550]g (18[20]oz) four-ply yarn
1 pair each 3mm (US3) and 3¼mm (US4) needles

TENSION
25 sts and 32 rows to 10cm (4in) over st st on 3¼mm (US4) needles.

FRONT AND BACK (one piece)
Beg at the lower edge of the front of the sweater, using 3mm (US3) needles, cast on 120[126] sts.
Work 9 rows g st.
Change to 3¼mm (US4) needles and work in st st, beg with a K row, until front measures 50[52]cm (19½[20½]in) from cast-on edge, ending with a WS row.

Divide for neck
Next row K60[63] sts, turn, leaving rem sts on a spare needle and cont on these sts only for left side of neck.
**Dec 1 st at neck edge of next and every foll 4th row until 30[33] sts rem.
Work 1 row (this point marks the shoulder line).
Now inc 1 st at neck edge of next and every foll 4th row until there are 60[63] sts, ending at neck edge.** Leave these sts on a spare needle.
With RS facing, rejoin yarn to sts on first spare needle. 60[63] sts.
Work 1 row.
Now work right side to match left from ** to **.
Cont to work across all 120[126] sts on both needles to join right and left side of back.
Cont in st st until back measures same as front from shoulder line to g st border, ending with a RS row.
Change to 3mm (US3) needles and work 9 rows g st.
Cast off.

SLEEVES
Beg at shoulder edge, using 3¼mm (US4) needles, cast on 125[131] sts.
Work in st st, dec 1 st at each end of every foll 4th row until there are 73[79] sts.
Work straight until sleeve measures 40[42]cm (16[16½]in) from cast-on edge, ending with a RS row.
Next row P3[6], *P2 tog, P3; rep from * to last 5[9] sts, P2tog, P3[6]. 59[65] sts.
Change to 3mm (US3) needles and work 2cm (¾in) in K1, P1 rib.
Cast off in rib.

MAKING UP
Neckband
Using 3mm (US3) needles, beg at point of back 'V', with RS facing K up 131 sts evenly along left back neck edge and left front neck edge.
Beg 1st row K1, work 6cm (2½in) K1, P1 rib, dec 2 sts at each end of every alt row as foll:
Decrease rows P1, sl 1, K2 tog, psso, rib to last 4 sts, K3 tog, P1.
Cast off in rib.
Work band on right side of neck to match.
Join neckband seams at front and back.
Set sleeves in flat, matching centre of cast-on edge of sleeve to shoulder line.
Join side and sleeve seams.

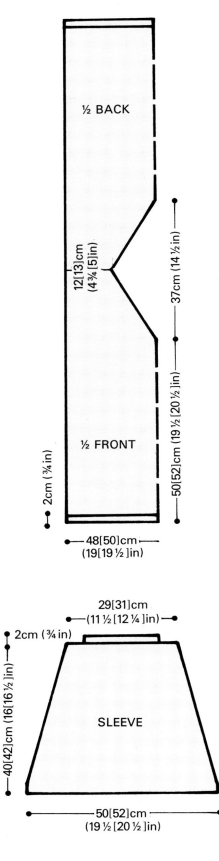

½ BACK

12[13]cm (4¾[5]in)

37cm (14½in)

½ FRONT

2cm (¾in)

50[52]cm (19½[20½]in)

48[50]cm (19[19½]in)

29[31]cm (11½[12¼]in)

2cm (¾in)

40[42]cm (16[16½]in)

SLEEVE

50[52]cm (19½[20½]in)

Designed by Soyzic Cornu Photograph: Mike Yavel

Trompe l'Oeuil

This deceptive little outfit is actually one sweater worked in three colours in fine cotton yarn.

SIZE
To fit 81–91cm (32–36in) bust

MATERIALS
250g (9oz) four-ply yarn in main colour (A)
200g (8oz) in 1st contrast colour (B)
50g (2oz) in 2nd contrast colour (C)
1 pair each 3mm (US3) and 3¼mm (US4) needles

TENSION
24 sts and 29 rows to 10cm (4in) over st st on 3¼mm (US4) needles.

FRONT
Using 3¼mm (US4) needles and A, cast on 114 sts.
Change to 3mm (US3) needles.
Work 14 rows in st st beg with a P row.
Change to 3¼mm (US4) needles.
K 1 row to form foldline.
Work 14 rows in st st beg with a K row.
Form hem
Next row Fold hem on to WS along foldline and K each st tog with corresponding st in cast-on edge.
Cont in st st in A until work measures 29cm (11½in) from hemline, ending with a WS row.
Commence patt from chart, using separate balls of yarn for each colour and twisting yarn between colours to avoid holes, as foll:
1st row (RS) K2B, 110A, 2B.
2nd row P4B, 106A, 4B.
Cont in this way, working LH half of front as a mirror image of RH half, work 3rd–20th rows from chart.
Shape armholes
Dec 1 st at each end of next and foll 5 alt rows. 102 sts.*
Now work straight until 56th row of chart has been worked, ending with a WS row.
Divide for neck
Next row Patt 47 sts, turn, leaving rem sts on a spare needle and cont on these sts only for left side of front.
**Cast off 3 sts at beg of next row and 2 sts at beg of foll 2 alt rows.
Work 1 row.
Now dec 1 st at neck edge on next and 8 foll alt rows. 31 sts.
Work 2 rows straight, thus ending with a WS row.
Cast off.
With RS facing, return to sts on spare needle, sl next 8 sts on to stitch holder, then rejoin yarn to next st and patt to end of row.
Work 1 row.
Complete right side to match left working from ** to end.

BACK
Work as given for the front of the sweater to *.
Now work straight until 78th row of chart has been worked, ending with a WS row.
Divide for neck
Next row Patt 42 sts as set, turn, leaving rem sts on a spare needle and then cont on these sts only for the right side of the neck.
Work 1 row.

Next row Patt 31 sts, turn, leaving rem 11 sts on a stitch holder.
Work 1 row.
Cast off.
With RS of work facing, return to sts on spare needle, sl next 18 sts on to stitch holder, rejoin yarn to next st, patt to end.
Next row Patt 31 sts, turn, leaving rem 11 sts on a stitch holder.
Work 1 row.
Cast off.

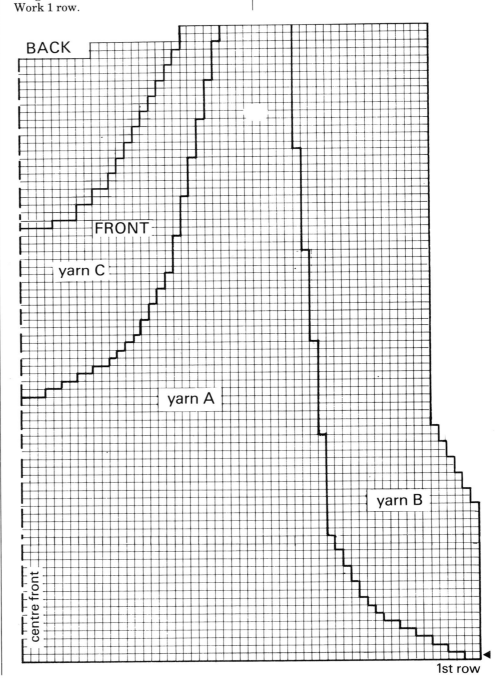

BACK

FRONT

yarn C

yarn A

yarn B

centre front

1st row

Designed by Valérie Ribadeau Dumas Photograph: Sepp

Trompe l'Oeuil

SLEEVES

Using 3¼mm (US4) needles and B, cast on 86 sts.
Change to 3mm (US3) needles and work 10 rows in st st beg with a P row.
Change to 3¼mm (US4) needles.
K 1 row to form hemline.
Work 10 rows st st beg with a K row.
Form hem as given for front.
Cont in st st in B, inc 1 st at each end of 7 foll 7th rows. 100 sts.
Now work straight until sleeve measures 22cm (8½in) from hemline, ending with a WS row.

Shape top

Dec 1 st at each end of next and 3 foll alt rows. 92 sts.
Work 1 row. Cast off.

MAKING UP

Join right shoulder seam.

Neckband

Using 3mm (US3) needles, with RS facing K up 16 sts down left side of front neck, K 8 sts from stitch holder, K up 16 sts up right side of front neck, K 40 sts from stitch holders at back neck. 80 sts.
Work 6 rows in st st, beg with a P row.
K 1 row for fold line.
Work 6 rows in st st beg with a K row.
Cast off loosely.
Join left shoulder and neckband seam.
Fold neckband on to WS along foldline and catch down to neck edge.
Join side seams leaving 5cm (2in) slits at hem edge.
Join sleeve seams and set in sleeves.

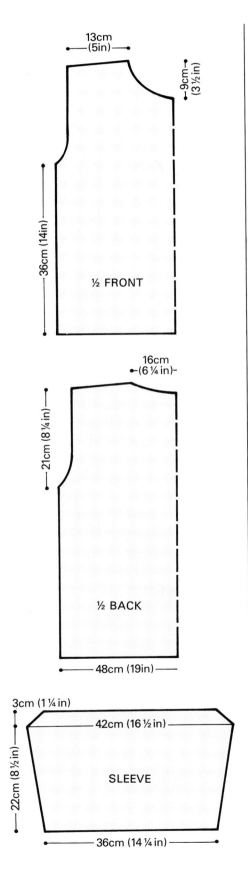

Lace and Cables

This gorgeous collection of cables and lacy patterns presents quite a challenge, but it's cunningly constructed to make the most of these marvellous stitches so the results will make any extra efforts undoubtedly worthwhile.

SUMMER
★ ★ ★

SIZES
To fit 81[86,91]cm (32[34,36]in) bust

MATERIALS
350[400,450]g (13[15,16]oz)
Aran-weight yarn
1 pair each 4½mm (US7) and 5½mm (US9) needles

TENSION
19 sts and 25 rows to 10cm (4in) over patt on 5½mm (US9) needles.

SPECIAL ABBREVIATIONS
C4B (cable 4 back)—sl next 2 sts on to cable needle and hold at back of work, K2, then K2 from cable needle.
C4F (cable 4 front)—sl next 2 sts on to cable needle and hold at front of work, K2, then K2 from cable needle.

PATT A
Worked over a multiple of 12 sts, plus 4 extra.
1st row (RS) P4, *K8, P4; rep from *.
2nd row K4, *P8, K4; rep from * to end.
3rd row P4, *C4B, C4F, P4; rep from * to end.
4th row As 2nd row.
5th row As 1st row.
6th row As 2nd row.
Rep 1st–6th rows.

PATT B
Worked over a multiple of 10 sts, plus 1 extra. See chart 1 on page 38.

PATT C
1st row (RS) P6, *K4, P1, K4, P5[6,7]; rep from * to last 1[0,15] sts, P1[0, end last rep P6].
2nd and every alt row K the P sts and P the K sts of previous row.
3rd row P6, *C4B, P1, C4F, P5[6,7]; rep from * to last 1[0,15] sts, P1[0, end last rep P6].
5th row As 1st row.
7th row P6, *yon, sl 1, K1, psso, K2, P1, K2, sl 1, K1, psso, yrn, P5[6,7]; rep from * to last 1[0,15] sts, P1[0, end last rep P6].
9th row P6, *P1, yon, sl 1, K1, psso, K1, P1, K1, K2 tog, yrn, P6[7,8]; rep from * to last 1[0,15] sts, P1[0, end last rep P7].
11th row P6, *P2, yon, sl 1, K1, psso, P1, K2 tog, yrn, P7[8,9]; rep from * to last 1[0,15] sts, P1[0, end last rep P8].
13th row P6, *P3, yon, sl 1, K2 tog, psso, yrn, P8[9,10]; rep from * to last 1[0,15] sts, P1[0, end last rep P9].
15th row P to end.
16th row K to end.
Work 1st–16th rows only.

PATT D
Worked over a multiple of 12 sts.
1st row (RS) P to end.
2nd row K to end.
3rd row *P4, K2, P1, K2, P3; rep from * to end.
4th row K the P sts and P the K sts of previous row.
5th row *P3, K2 tog, K1, yrn, P1, yon, K1, sl 1, P1, psso, P2; rep from * to end.
6th row * K2, P2, K1, K into front, back and front again of next st then lift 2nd and 3rd sts over 1st st and off needle to make bobble, K1, P2, K3; rep from * to end.
7th row P2, K2 tog, K1, yrn, P3, yon, K1, sl 1, P1, psso; rep from * to end.
8th row As 4th row.
9th row *P1, K2 tog, K1, yrn, P5, yon, K1, sl 1, K1, psso; rep from * to end.
10th row As 4th row.
11th row P to end.
12th row K to end.
Work 1st–12th rows only.

PATT E
1st row (RS) *K2, P2; rep from * to end.
2nd row As 1st row.
Work 1st–2nd rows only.

PATT F
Finish cables formed by patt A working from 5th row of chart 2 to end.

SLEEVE PATT SEQUENCE

rows	patt
1(WS)	K to end
2–7	B
8–9	st st
10–25	C
26–7	st st
28–9	rev st st
30–31	st st
32–43	D
44–5	st st
46–7	E
48–9	st st
50–51	rev st st
52–79[85,91]	A
80[86,92]–87[93,99]	F

Lace and Cables

FRONT
Using 4½mm (US7) needles, cast on 78[82,86] sts.
Work 3cm (1¼in) K1, P1 rib.
Cont in rib, cast off 19[21,23] sts at beg of next 2 rows. 40 sts.
Change to 5½mm (US9) needles and work 37[39.5,42]cm (14½[15¾,16½]in) in patt A, ending with a WS row.
Divide for neck
Cont in patt A.
Next row Work 10 sts in patt A, turn, leaving rem sts on a spare needle and cont on these sts only for left side of neck.
Work 1 row.
**Next row* Patt 5 sts, turn, leaving rem 5 sts on a safety pin. 5 sts.
Work 1 row. Leave these sts on a safety pin.**
With RS facing, return to sts left on spare needle, sl next 20 sts on to stitch holder, rejoin yarn to next st, patt to end.
Work to match left side from ** to **.
Neckband
Using 4½mm (US7) needles, with RS facing sl all 40 sts left at neck edge on to needle.
Work in K1, P1 rib as foll:
Next row Rib 2, K up loop between last st and next st to make 1, (rib 3, make 1) twice, rib 24, (make 1, rib 3) twice, make 1, rib 2. 46 sts.
Cont in rib until neckband measures 1cm (½in). Cast off in rib.

BACK
Work as given for front.

LEFT SIDE AND SLEEVE
Using 5½mm (US9) needles, with RS facing K up 80[85,90] sts along left side of front, beg at cast-off edge of lower rib, cast on 1 st, then K up 80[85,90] sts along left side of back beg at cast-off edge of neckband. 161[171,181] sts.
Work in patt foll sleeve patt sequence (page 37), *at the same time* shape side and sleeve as foll:
Work 10[11,12]cm (4[4½,5]in) straight.
Shape sleeve
Cast off 10 sts at beg of next 8[6,6] rows then 0[12,14] sts at beg of next 0[2,2] rows. Now dec 1 st at each end of foll 4[5,6] alt rows, then 1 st at each end of 9 foll 4th rows. 55[59,63] sts.
Work straight until 87[93,99] rows in sleeve patt sequence have been completed, ending with a WS row.
Next row P to end.
Next row K to end.
Change to 4½mm (US7) needles.
Work 3cm (1¼in) K2, P2 rib.
Cast off in rib.

RIGHT SIDE AND SLEEVE
Using 5½mm (US9) needles, with RS facing K up 80[85,90] sts along right side of back beg at cast-off edge of lower rib, cast on 1 st, then K up 80[85,90] sts along right side of front beg at cast-off edge of neckband. 161[171,181] sts.
Complete right side and sleeve as given for left side and sleeve.

MAKING UP
Join lower ribs on front and back to left and right sides.
Join side and sleeve seams.

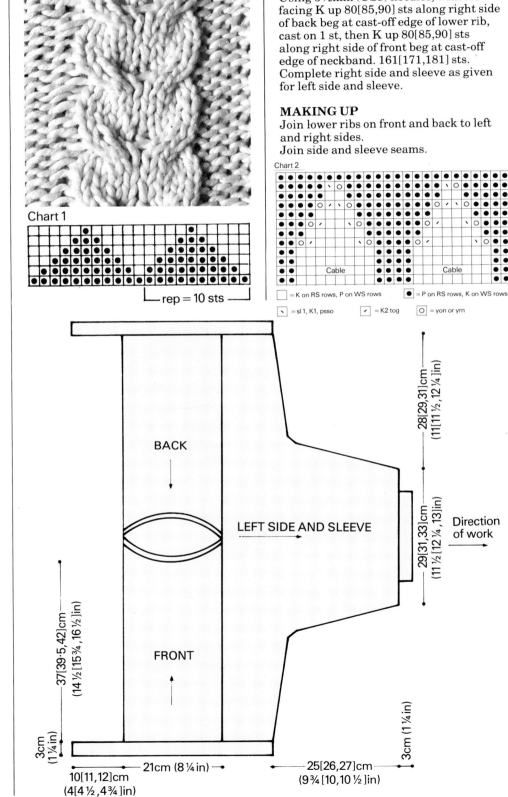

Chart 1

rep = 10 sts

Chart 2

□ = K on RS rows, P on WS rows   ● = P on RS rows, K on WS rows

╲ = sl 1, K1, psso   ╱ = K2 tog   O = yon or yrn

Cable

BACK

LEFT SIDE AND SLEEVE

Direction of work

FRONT

28[29,31]cm (11[11½,12¼]in)

29[31,33]cm (11½[12¼,13]in)

37[39.5,42]cm (14½[15¾,16½]in)

3cm (1¼in)

21cm (8¼in)

10[11,12]cm (4[4½,4¾]in)

25[26,27]cm (9¾[10,10½]in)

3cm (1¼in)

Designed by Soyzic Cornu Photograph: Sepp

All Gold

Silky rayon yarn gives this loose T-shaped sweater a floppy, easy feeling but it would work well in many different yarns—smooth wool, slubbed linen, even mohair.

SUMMER ★

SIZES
To fit 81[86,91]cm (32[34,36]in) bust

MATERIALS
500[500,550]g (18[18,20]oz) double knitting yarn
1 pair each 3mm (US3) and 4mm (US6) needles

TENSION
23 sts and 30 rows to 10cm (4in) over st st on 4mm (US6) needles.

FRONT
Using 3mm (US3) needles, cast on 120 [124,128] sts.
Work 2cm (¾in) K1, P1 rib.
Change to 4mm (US6) needles and work in st st until front measures 44[46,48]cm (17½[18,19]in) from top of rib, ending with a WS row.
Divide for neck
Next row K51[53,55], turn, leaving rem sts on a spare needle and cont on these sts only for left side of neck.
Cast off 2 sts at beg of next and foll 5 alt rows. 39[41,43] sts.
Shape shoulder
Cast off 13[13,15] sts at beg of next row and then cast off 13[14,14] sts at beg of foll alt row.
Work 1 row.
Cast off rem 13[14,14] sts.
With RS facing, rejoin yarn to sts on spare needle, cast off 18 sts, K to end of row.
Complete the second side of neck to match the first side of neck, reversing shapings.

BACK
Work as given for front.

SLEEVES
Using 3mm (US3) needles, cast on 78 [82,88] sts.
Work 3cm (1¼in) K1, P1 rib.
Change to 4mm (US6) needles and work in st st, inc 1 st at each end of every foll 3rd row until there are 110[114,120] sts on needle.
Now work straight until sleeve measures 23[24,25]cm (9[9½,9¾]in) from top of rib.
Cast off.

MAKING UP
Join shoulder seams.
Set sleeves in flat, matching the centre of the cast-off edge of sleeve to the shoulder seam.
Join side and sleeve seams.
Turn under 1cm (½in) around neck edge and stitch down.

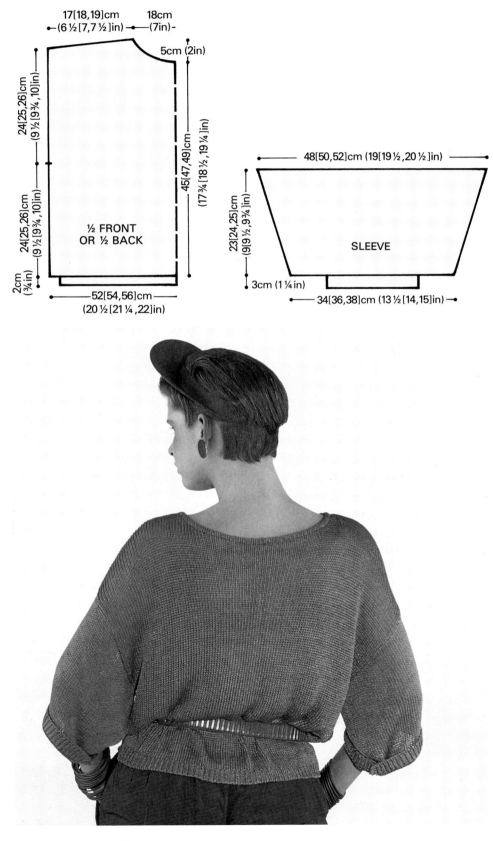

17[18,19]cm
←(6½[7,7½]in)→
18cm
(7in)
5cm (2in)
24[25,26]cm
(9½[9¾,10]in)
45[47,49]cm
(17¾[18½,19¼]in)
½ FRONT OR ½ BACK
24[25,26]cm
(9½[9¾,10]in)
2cm
(¾in)
52[54,56]cm
(20½[21¼,22]in)

48[50,52]cm (19[19½,20½]in)
23[24,25]cm
(9[9½,9¾]in)
SLEEVE
3cm (1¼in)
34[36,38]cm (13½[14,15]in)

Designed by Jacqueline Jacobson for Dorothée Bis Photograph: Sepp

Cool Customer

This cotton sweater is knitted entirely in one piece, beginning at the right cuff. When worked in this way from side to side, the stitch creates a ladder-like effect, which helps to make it very cool to wear.

SIZE
To fit 81–91cm (32–36in) bust

MATERIALS
400g (15oz) four-ply yarn
1 pair 2¾mm (US2) and 3¼mm (US4) needles
1 set four 2¾mm (US2) double-pointed needles

TENSION
23 sts and 33 rows to 10cm (4in) over patt on 3¼mm (US4) needles.

TO MAKE (one piece)
Beg at right cuff, using 2¾mm (US2) needles, cast on 61 sts.
K 2 rows.
Change to 3¼mm (US3) needles and commence patt as foll, *at the same time* inc 1 st at each end of 8th row:
1st row (WS) K to end.
2nd row K to end, winding yarn twice round needle on each st.
3rd row K to end, dropping extra loop on each st.
4th–10th rows Work in moss st.
These 10 rows form the patt rep.
Cont in patt, inc 1 st at each end of every 8th row from previous inc until there are 95 sts.
Work 13 rows straight, ending with a WS row.
Shape front and back
Cast on 50 sts at beg of next 2 rows. 195 sts.
Work straight until work measures 16cm (6¼in) from beg of back and front shaping, ending with a WS row.
Divide for neck
Next row Patt 96 sts, K2 tog, patt to end.
Next row Patt 97 sts, turn, leaving rem sts on a spare needle and cont on these sts only for back.
Work 66 rows straight, ending at neck edge. Leave these sts on a spare needle.
With WS facing rejoin yarn to sts left on first spare needle and cont on these sts for front.
Keeping patt correct, dec 1 st at neck edge on next 4 rows, then 1 st at same edge on foll 5 alt rows, and 1 st at same edge on 2 foll 4th rows. 86 sts.
Now work 23 rows straight.
Inc 1 st at neck edge on next and 2 foll 4th rows, then 1 st at same edge on 5 foll alt rows and then at same edge on foll 3 rows.
Join front and back
Next row Patt 96 sts, inc 1 in next st, patt across 97 sts left on second spare needle. 195 sts.
Now work straight until work measures

16cm (6¼in) from end of neck shaping, ending with a WS row.
Shape left sleeve
Cast off 50 sts at beg of next 2 rows. 95 sts.
Dec 1 st at each end of 14th and every foll 8th row until there are 61 sts. Work 7 rows straight.
Change to 2¾mm (US2) needles.
K 2 rows. Cast off.

MAKING UP
Neckband
With RS facing, using double-pointed 2¾mm (US2) needles, K up 132 sts evenly around neck edge.
Work 4 rounds g st. Cast off.
Lower edgings
Using 2¾mm (US2) needles, with RS facing K up 140 sts along lower front edge.
Work 4 rows g st. Cast off.
Make similar border for back.
Join side and sleeve seams.

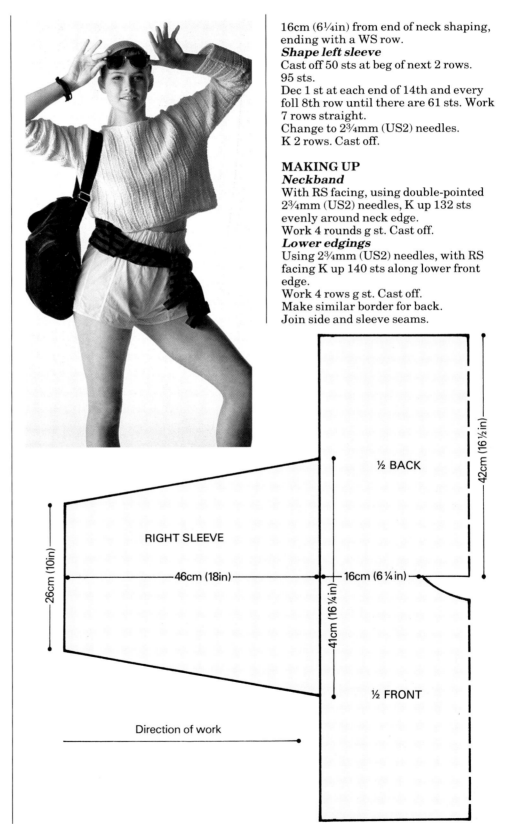

½ BACK

42cm (16½in)

RIGHT SLEEVE

26cm (10in)

46cm (18in)

16cm (6¼in)

41cm (16¼in)

½ FRONT

Direction of work

53cm (21in)

Designed by Valérie Ribadeau Dumas   Photograph: François Pomepui

Le Rouge

This straightforward T-shirt is worked in a lightly textured rib stitch. There is very little shaping which makes it extremely easy and quick to knit.

SIZES
To fit 81[86,91]cm (32[34,36]in) bust

MATERIALS
600[650,700]g (22[23,25]oz) chunky yarn
1 pair each 4½mm (US7) and 7mm (US10½) needles

TENSION
17 sts and 23 rows to 10cm (4in) over patt on 7mm (US10½) needles.

FRONT
Using 4½mm (US7) needles, cast on 70[74,78] sts.
Work 5cm (2in) K2, P2 rib, inc 11 sts evenly across last row. 81[85,89] sts.
Change to 7mm (US10½) needles and commence patt.
1st row (RS) K1, *K1, P1, K2; rep from * to end.
2nd row P1, *K3, P1; rep from * to end.
These 2 rows form the patt rep.
Cont in patt until work measures 45[47,49]cm (17¾[18½,19¼]in) from top of rib.
Work 3cm (1¼in) in K2, P2 rib, dec 1 st in middle of 1st row.
Cast off in rib.

BACK
Work as given for front.

SLEEVES
Beg at shoulder, using 7mm (US10½) needles, cast on 89[93,97] sts.
Work 5[7,9] rows in patt as given for front.
Cont in patt dec 1 st at each end of next and every foll 4th row until 59[63,67] sts rem.
Now work straight until sleeve measures 28[29,30]cm (11[11½,12]in) from cast-on edge, ending with a WS row.
Change to 4½mm (US7) needles and work 2cm (¾in) K2, P2 rib, dec 1 st in middle of 1st row.
Cast off in rib.

MAKING UP
Join shoulder seams to 14[15,16]cm (5½[6,6¼]in) in from each side.
Set sleeves in flat matching centre of cast-on edge of sleeve to shoulder seam.
Join side and sleeve seams.

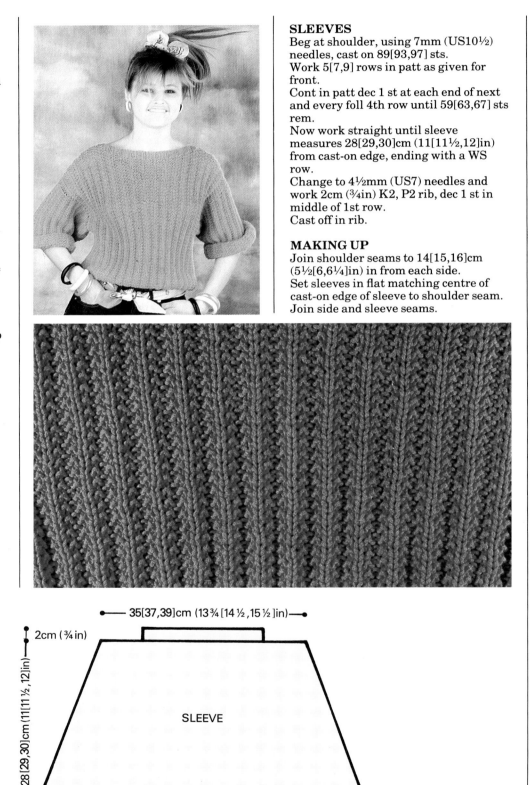

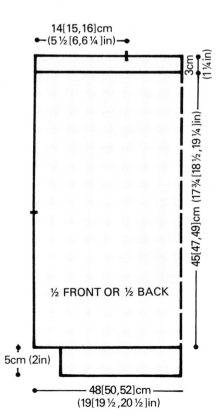

14[15,16]cm
(5 ½[6,6 ¼]in)

3cm
(1¼in)

45[47,49]cm (17¾[18½,19 ¼]in)

½ FRONT OR ½ BACK

5cm (2in)

48[50,52]cm
(19[19 ½,20 ½]in)

35[37,39]cm (13 ¾ [14 ½ ,15 ½]in)

2cm (¾ in)

28[29,30]cm (11[11 ½ ,12]in)

SLEEVE

52[55,57]cm (20 ½ [21¾ ,22 ½]in)

Designed by Soyzic Cornu Photograph: Sepp

Sun Top

Perfect for the beach—a cool cotton vest knitted in moss stitch with hemmed and garter-stitch edges.

SIZE
To fit 81–91cm (32–36in) bust

MATERIALS
150g (6oz) double knitting yarn
1 pair 3mm (US3) needles
1 5mm (US8) needle

TENSION
22 sts and 29 rows to 10cm (4in) over moss st using one 3mm (US3) and one 5mm (US8) needle.

FRONT
Using pair 3mm (US3) needles, cast on 103 sts.
Work 2.5cm (1in) st st, ending with a K row.
K 1 row for foldline.
Beg with a K row, work 2.5cm (1in) st st, ending with a P row.
Change to a single 3mm (US3) needle with a single 5mm (US8) needle and work in moss st as foll:
1st row (RS) (K1, P1) to last st, K1.
Rep this row.
Cont in moss st until work measures 23cm (9in) from cast-on edge, ending with a WS row.**
Shape armholes and divide for neck
Next row Cast off 6 sts, patt 42 including st used to cast off, turn, leaving rem sts on a spare needle and cont on these sts only for first side of neck.
Next row Cast off 5 sts, patt to end.
Cont to shape armhole casting off 6 sts at beg next and foll alt row, then 5 sts, 3 sts, 2 sts and 1 st on foll 4 alt rows, *at the same time* shape neck by casting off 4 sts at beg of next alt row and 3 sts, 2 sts and 1 st at beg of foll 3 alt rows. 4 sts.
Now work straight until front measures 22cm (8½in) from beg of armhole shaping.
Cast off.
With RS of work facing, rejoin yarn to sts left on spare needle, cast off 7 sts, patt to end.
Next row Cast off 6 sts, patt to end.
Complete second side of neck to match first side, reversing shapings.

BACK
Work as given for front to **.
Shape armholes
Cast off 6 sts at beg of next 6 rows and 5 sts at beg of foll 2 rows.
Divide for neck
Next row Cast off 3 sts, patt 20 sts including st used to cast off, turn, leaving rem sts on a spare needle and cont on these sts only for first side of neck.

Cast off 5 sts at beg of next row, and 4 sts at beg of foll alt row, *at the same time* cont to shape armhole by casting off 2 sts at beg of next alt row and 1 st at beg of foll alt row. 8 sts.
Now cast off 2 sts at neck edge on next row and dec 1 st on same edge on foll 2 alt rows.
Work straight until back matches front to cast-off edge.
Cast off rem 4 sts.
With RS of work facing, rejoin yarn to sts left on spare needle, cast off 11 sts, patt to end.
Next row Cast off 3 sts, patt to end of row.
Complete second side to match first side, reversing shapings.

MAKING UP
Join right shoulder seam very neatly.
Neck edging
With RS of work facing, using pair 3mm (US3) needles, K up 220 sts evenly around neck edge.
Work 3 rows g st.
Cast off.
Join left shoulder seam.
Armhole edgings
With RS of work facing, using pair 3mm (US3) needles, K up 140 sts evenly around armhole edge.
Work 3 rows g st.
Cast off.
Join side seams.
Fold under lower hem along foldline and catch down neatly to WS.

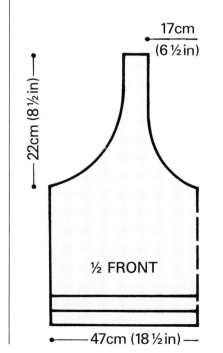

17cm (6½in)

22cm (8½in)

½ FRONT

47cm (18½in)

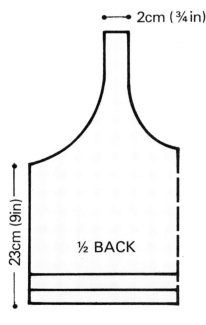

2cm (¾in)

23cm (9in)

½ BACK

Designed by Valérie Ribadeau Dumas Photograph: Sepp

Skinny Vest

Great for sun-worshippers, a skimpy vest knitted in fine cotton. The stitch is a close mesh worked on one small and one medium-sized needle.

SIZE
To fit 81cm (32in) bust

MATERIALS
100g (4oz) four-ply yarn in main colour (A)
25g (1oz) in contrast colour (B)
1 pair each 2¼mm (US1) and 4mm (US6) needles
1 2¼mm (US1) circular needle

TENSION
27 sts and 45 rows to 10cm (4in) over mesh patt using one 2¼mm (US1) and one 4mm (US6) needle.

FRONT
Using 2¼mm (US1) needles and A, cast on 110 sts.
Work 6 rows g st.
Change to one 2¼mm (US1) and one 4mm (US6) needle and commence mesh patt:
1st row (WS) With 2¼mm (US1) needle, K1, *K1, yfwd, sl 1 P-wise tbl, ybk; rep from * to last st, K1.
2nd row With 4mm (US6) needle, P to end.
3rd row With 2¼mm (US1) needle, K1, *yfwd, sl 1 P-wise tbl, ybk, K1; rep from * to last st, K1.
4th row As 2nd row.
These 4 rows form the patt rep.
Cont in mesh patt until work measures 21cm (8¼in) from cast-on edge, ending with a WS row.**
Shape armholes
Cast off 5 sts at beg of next 2 rows, then 3 sts at beg of foll 4 rows and 2 sts at beg of foll 6 rows. Now dec 1 st at each end of next and foll alt row. 72 sts.
Divide for neck
Next row Patt 31 sts, turn, leaving rem sts on a spare needle and cont on these sts only for right side of neck.
Cont to shape armhole by dec 1 st at armhole edge on next and 11 foll alt rows, *at the same time* shape neck by casting off 3 sts at beg of next row and 2 sts at beg of foll alt row, then dec 1 st at neck edge on 3 foll alt rows, then on 4 foll 4th rows and 6 foll 6th rows. 1 st. Fasten off.
With WS of work facing, rejoin yarn to sts left on spare needle, cast off 10 sts, patt to end. 31 sts.
Complete left side to match right side, reversing shapings.

BACK
Work as given for front to **.
Shape armholes
Cast off 5 sts at beg of next 2 rows, then 3 sts at beg of foll 4 rows. 88 sts.

Divide for neck
Next row Cast off 2 sts, patt 39 sts, including st used to cast off, turn, leaving rem sts on a spare needle and cont on these sts only for first side of neck.
Cast off 3 sts at beg of next row, and 2 sts at beg of foll 3 rows. Now dec 1 st at neck edge on next and 2 foll alt rows, then on 6 foll 4th rows and 6 foll 6th rows, *at the same time* dec 1 st at armhole edge on 6 foll alt rows, then on 8 foll 4th rows. 1 st. Fasten off.
Rejoin yarn to sts on spare needle, cast off centre 6 sts, patt to end.
Next row Cast off 2 sts, patt to end. 39 sts.
Complete to match first side of neck, reversing shapings.

MAKING UP
Neck edging
Using 2¼mm (US1) circular needle and yarn B, with RS of work facing, K up 126 sts around front neck edge, turn and cast on 65 sts for right shoulder strap, K up 112 sts around back neck, turn and cast on 65 sts for left shoulder strap. 368 sts.
K 1 row. Cast off.
Armhole edging
Using 2¼mm (US1) needles and yarn B, with RS of work facing, K up 130 sts around armhole edge.
K 1 row. Cast off.
Join left shoulder strap to front neck edge.
Join side seams.

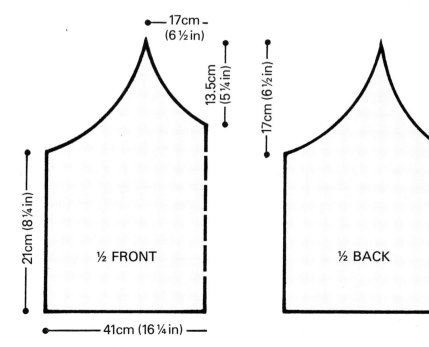

17cm (6½in)

13.5cm (5¼in)

21cm (8¼in)

½ FRONT

41cm (16¼in)

17cm (6½in)

16cm (6¼in)

½ BACK

Designed by Valérie Ribadeau Dumas Photograph: François Pomepui

Cabled Shift

A combination of cables and Irish moss stitch add a pleasing texture to this cool summer top. Knitted in tweedy wool, for example, the same pattern would make a superb loose slipover for winter.

SIZES
To fit 81[86,91]cm (32[34,36]in) bust

MATERIALS
500[550,600]g (18[20,22]oz) double knitting yarn
1 pair each 4mm (US6) and 4½mm (US7) needles

TENSION
22 sts and 28 rows to 10cm (4in) over reverse st st on 4½mm (US7) needles.

PANEL PATT A
Worked over 6 sts.
1st row (RS) K to end.
2nd and every alt row P to end.
3rd row Sl next 3 sts on to cable needle and hold at back of work, K3, then K3 from cable needle.
5th and 7th rows K to end.
9th row As 3rd row.
11th, 13th, 15th and 17th rows K to end.
18th row As 2nd row.
These 18 rows form the patt rep.

PANEL PATT B
Worked over 2 sts.
1st row (RS) K into front of 2nd st on LH needle, then into front of 1st st, dropping both sts off needle at the same time.
2nd row P to end.
Rep these 2 rows.

FRONT
Using 4mm (US6) needles, cast on 80[84, 88] sts. Work 6cm (2½in) in K1, P1 rib.
Next row Rib to end, inc 22 sts evenly across row. 102[106,110] sts.
Change to 4½mm (US7) needles and commence patt as foll:
1st row (RS) P7[9,11], work 1st row of panel patt B, P8, work 1st row panel patt A, P8, work 1st row of panel patt B, P6, K2, (K1, P1) 10 times, K2, P6, work 1st row of panel patt B, P8, work 1st row of panel patt A, P8, work 1st row of panel patt B, P7[9,11].
2nd row K7[9,11], work 2nd row panel patt B, K8, work 2nd row panel patt A, K8, work 2nd row panel patt B, K6, P2, (K1, P1) 10 times, P2, K6, work 2nd row panel patt B, K8, work 2nd row panel patt A, K8, work 2nd row panel patt B, K7[9,11].
3rd row P7[9,11], work 1st row panel patt B, P8, work 3rd row panel patt A, P8, work 1st row panel patt B, P6, K2, (P1, K1) 10 times, K2, P6, work 1st row panel patt B, P8, work 3rd row panel patt A, P8, work 1st row panel patt B, P7[9,11].

4th row K7[9,11], work 2nd row panel patt B, K8, work 4th row panel patt A, K8, work 2nd row panel patt B, K6, P2, (P1, K1) 10 times, P2, K6, work 2nd row panel patt B, K8, work 4th row panel patt A, K8, work 2nd row panel patt B, K7[9,11].
These 4 rows establish the position of the panel patts. Rep these 4 rows but working the appropriate rows of panel patt *at the same time* inc 1 st at each end of every 7th row until there are 118[122,126] sts.*
Now work straight until front measures 40[42,44]cm (16[16½,17½]in) from top of rib, ending with a WS row.
Divide for neck
Next row Patt 36[38,40] sts, turn, leaving rem sts on a spare needle and cont on these sts only for left side neck.
Dec 1 st at beg of next and foll 4 alt rows. 31[33,35] sts.
Work straight until front measures 47[49,51]cm (18½[19,20]in) from top of rib, ending with a WS row. Break yarn.
Leave these sts on a spare needle.
With RS facing, return to sts left on first spare needle, sl next 46 sts on to stitch holder, patt to end. 36[38,40] sts.
Complete to match left side of neck reversing shaping.

BACK
Work as given for front to *.
Now work straight until back measures 45[47,49]cm (17¾[18½,19¼]in) from top

of rib, ending with a WS row.
Divide for neck
Next row Patt 31[33,35] sts, turn, leaving rem sts on a spare needle, cont on these sts only for left side of neck.
Work straight until back measures 47[49,51]cm (18½[19,20]in) from top of rib, ending with a WS row.
Leave these sts on a spare needle. With RS of work facing, rejoin yarn to sts on spare needle, sl next 56 sts on to stitch holder, patt to end. 31[33,35] sts.
Complete to match RS of neck, reversing shapings.

MAKING UP
Graft right shoulder seam.
Neckband
Using 4mm (US6) needles, with RS facing, K up 10 sts down left side of neck, K 46 from spare needle, K up 10 up right side of neck, K up 5 down right side of back neck, K56 from spare needle, K up 5 up left side of back neck. 132 sts.
Work 2cm (¾in) in K1, P1 rib.
Cast off in rib. Graft left shoulder seam.
Join neckband seam.
Armbands
Mark position of armholes 24[25,26]cm (9½[9¾,10]in) below shoulder seams.
Using 4mm (US6) needles, with RS facing, K up 94[98,102] sts along armhole edge on each side of shoulder seam. 188[196,204] sts. Work 5cm (2in) in K2, P2 rib. Cast off in rib.
Join side and armband seams.

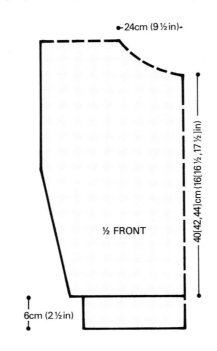

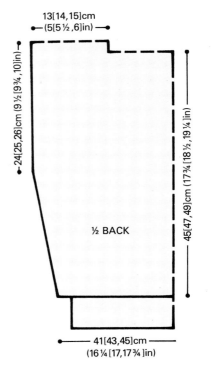

Designed by Anke Tikhomiroff Photograph: François Pompui

Borderline

A stylish, simple sweater with a fashionably wide, waist-length shape and deep sleeves. It's knitted in stocking stitch with contrasting striped borders.

SIZE
To fit 81–91cm (32–36in) bust

MATERIALS
600g (22oz) Aran-weight yarn in main colour (A)
100g (4oz) Aran-weight yarn in contrast colour (B)
1 pair each 4mm (US6) and 5mm (US8) needles

TENSION
14 sts and 20 rows to 10cm (4in) over st st on 5mm (US8) needles.

FRONT
Using 4mm (US6) needles and yarn A, cast on 76 sts.
Work 5cm (2in) K2, P2 rib as foll:
1st row (K2, P2) to end.
Rep this row.
P 1 row.
Change to 5mm (US8) needles and commence stripe patt:
1st row (RS) (K19B, 19A) twice.
2nd row (P19B, 19A) twice.
3rd row (K19A, 19B) twice.
4th row P to end in A.
5th row As 1st row.
6th row (P19A, 19B) twice.
7th–9th rows As 1st–3rd rows.
10th–11th rows As 2nd–3rd rows.
12th, 14th and 16th rows As 6th row.
13th and 15th rows As 1st row.
These 16 rows form the stripe patt.
Cont in st st in A only until work measures 20cm (8in) from top of rib, ending with a P row.
Shape armholes
Cast off 5 sts at beg of next 2 rows, now dec 1 st at each end of next and foll alt row. 62 sts.**
Now work straight until front measures 16cm (6¼in) from beg of armhole shaping, ending with a P row.
Divide for neck
Next row K28, turn, leaving rem sts on a spare needle and cont on these sts only for first side of neck.
Cast off 3 sts at beg of next row, then 2 sts at beg of foll 2 alt rows.
Work 1 row.
Now dec 1 st at neck edge on next and foll 3 alt rows. 17 sts.
Work straight until front measures 25cm (9¾in) from beg of armhole shaping, ending at armhole edge.
Cast off.
With RS facing rejoin yarn to sts on spare needle, cast off 6 sts, K to end. 28 sts.
Complete second side of neck to match first side of neck, reversing shapings.

BACK
Work as given for front to **.
Now work straight until back measures 2 rows less than front to shoulder, ending with a P row.
Divide for neck
Next row K20, turn, leaving rem sts on a spare needle and cont on these sts only for first side of neck.
Cast off 3 sts at beg of next row. 17 sts.
Cast off.
With RS facing rejoin yarn to sts left on spare needle, cast off 22 sts, K to end of row.
Complete second side of neck to match first side of neck, reversing shapings.

RIGHT SLEEVE
Using 4mm (US6) needles and yarn A, cast on 52 sts.
Work 5cm (2in) K2, P2 rib.
P 1 row.
Change to 5mm (US8) needles and commence stripe patt:
1st row (RS) K7B, 19A, 19B, 7A.
2nd row P7B, 19A, 19B, 7A.
3rd row K7A, 19B, 19A, 7B.
4th row P to end in A.
5th row As 1st row.
6th row P7A, 19B, 19A, 7B.
7th–16th rows Work as for front, *at the same time* inc 1 at each end of 8th and 16th rows. 56 sts.
Cont in st st in A only, inc 1 st at each end of every foll 6th row until there are 70 sts.
Work straight until sleeve measures 40cm (16in) from top of rib, ending with a P row.
Shape top
Cast off 3 sts at beg of next 2 rows, then 2 sts at beg of foll 4 rows. 56 sts.
Cast off.

LEFT SLEEVE
Work as given for right sleeve reversing stripe patt as foll:
1st row K7A, 19B, 19A, 7B.
2nd row P7A, 19B, 19A, 7B.
3rd row K7B, 19A, 19B, 7A.
Cont to reverse patt as set.

MAKING UP
Join right shoulder seam.
Neckband
Using 4mm (US6) needles and yarn A, with RS of work facing, K up 76 sts evenly around neck edge.
Work 2cm (¾in) K2, P2 rib.
Cast off in rib.
Join left shoulder and neckband seam.
Join side and sleeve seams.
Set in sleeves.

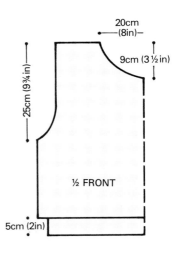

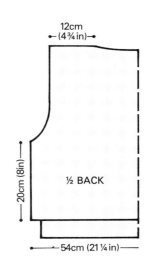

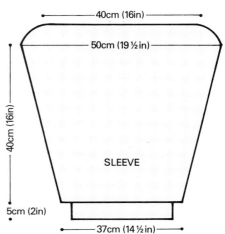

Designed by Valérie Ribadeau Dumas Photograph: François Pomepui

Chunky Rib

An interesting rib pattern and a thick tweedy yarn make something special of this simple sweater.

AUTUMN
★

SIZE
To fit 81–91cm (32–36in) bust

MATERIALS
600g (22oz) double knitting yarn
1 pair each 3¼mm (US4) and 4mm (US6) needles

TENSION
17 sts and 22 rows to 10cm (4in) over rib patt on 4mm (US6) needles.

FRONT
Using 3¼mm (US4) needles, cast on 93 sts.
Work 4 rows g st.
Commence rib patt:
1st row (K2, P2) to last st, K1.
This row forms the patt rep.
Work 9 more rows in rib patt.
Change to 4mm (US6) needles and cont in rib patt until work measures 27cm (10½in) from cast-on edge.
Shape armholes
Cast off 2 sts at beg of next 4 rows and 4 sts at beg of next 2 rows. 77 sts.**
Now work straight until front measures 17cm (6½in) from beg of armhole shaping, ending with a WS row.
Divide for neck
Next row Patt 34 sts, turn, leaving rem sts on a spare needle and cont on these sts only for first side of neck.
Cast off 5 sts at beg of next row and 3 sts at beg of foll 2 alt rows.

Now cast off 2 sts at beg of next 2 alt rows and dec 1 st at beg of foll 2 alt rows. 17 sts.
Work 4 rows straight, ending at armhole edge.
Shape shoulder
Cast off 6 sts at beg of next and foll alt row.
Work 1 row.
Cast off.
With RS facing rejoin yarn to sts on spare needle, cast off 9 sts, patt to end. 34 sts.
Complete to match first side of neck reversing shapings.

BACK
Work as given for front to **.
Now work straight until back measures same as front to shoulder.
Shape shoulders
Cast off 6 sts at beg of next 2 rows.
Divide for neck
Next row Cast off 6 sts, patt 14 sts including st used to cast off, turn, leaving rem sts on a spare needle and cont on these sts only for first side of neck.
Next row Cast off 9 sts, patt to end of row.
Cast off.
With RS facing rejoin yarn to sts on spare needle, cast off 25 sts, patt to end of row.
Cast off 6 sts at beg of next row and 9 sts

at beg of foll row.
Cast off rem 5 sts.

SLEEVES
Using 3¼mm (US4) needles, cast on 53 sts.
Work 4 rows g st, then 10 rows in rib patt as given for front.
Change to 4mm (US6) needles and cont in rib patt for 10cm (4in).
Cont in rib patt inc 1 st at each end of every foll 5th row until there are 77 sts on needle.
Now work straight until sleeve measures 47cm (18½in) from cast-on edge.
Shape top
Cast off 4 sts at beg of next 2 rows, then 3 sts at beg of foll 2 rows. Now cast off 2 sts at beg of next 4 rows.
Dec 1 st at each end of next and 5 foll alt rows. 43 sts.
Cast off.

MAKING UP
Join right shoulder seam.
Neckband
Using 3¼mm (US4) needles, with RS of work facing, K up 77 sts evenly around neck edge.
Work 4 rows g st.
Cast off.
Join left shoulder and neckband seam.
Join side and sleeve seams.
Set in sleeves.

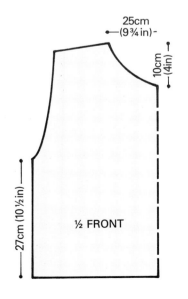

½ FRONT

25cm (9¾ in)
10cm (4in)
27cm (10½ in)

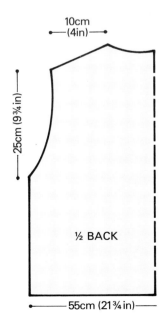

½ BACK

10cm (4in)
25cm (9¾ in)
55cm (21¾ in)

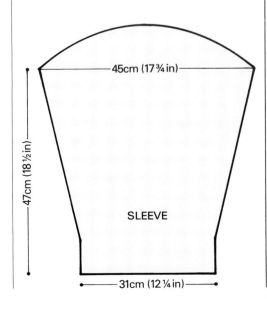

SLEEVE

45cm (17¾ in)
47cm (18½ in)
31cm (12¼ in)

Designed by Valérie Ribadeau Dumas Photograph: Sepp

Button-Up

A chunky coat knitted in thick wool in a fancy rib stitch pattern. Ideal for the great outdoors, right up until the first frosts.

SIZES
To fit 86[91,96]cm (34[36,38]in) bust

MATERIALS
1100[1150,1200]g (40[41,43]oz) Aran-weight yarn
1 pair each 4½mm (US7) and 5½mm (US9) needles
5 buttons

TENSION
20 sts and 23 rows to 10cm (4in) over rib patt on 5½mm (US9) needles.

RIGHT FRONT
Using 5½mm (US9) needles, cast on 46[48,50] sts.
Work 4cm (1½in) K1, P1 rib.
Commence rib patt:
1st row K1[2,1], P0[1,0], *K3, P1; rep from * to last st, K1.
This row forms the rib patt rep.
Cont in patt until work measures 37[38,39]cm (14½[15,15½]in) from top of K1, P1 rib, ending at armhole edge.
Shape armhole
Cast off 5 sts at beg of next row. 41[43,45] sts.
Work straight until front measures 22[23,24]cm (8½[9,9¾]in) from beg of armhole shaping, ending at neck edge.
Shape neck
Cast off 5 sts at beg of next row and 2 sts at beg of foll 2 alt rows then 1 st at beg of next 2 alt rows, ending at armhole edge. 30[32,34] sts.
Shape shoulder
Cast off 15[16,17] sts at beg of next row.

Work 1 row. Cast off rem 15[16,17] sts.

LEFT FRONT
Work as given for right front, reversing all shapings.

BACK
Using 5½mm (US9) needles, cast on 102[106,110] sts.
Work 4cm (1½in) K1, P1 rib.
Now work in rib patt as for 1st size of right front until work measures same as fronts to armhole.
Shape armholes
Cast off 5 sts at beg of next 2 rows. 92[96,100] sts.
Work straight until back matches fronts to shoulder.
Shape shoulders
Cast off 15[16,17] sts at beg of next 4 rows.
Cast off rem 32 sts.

SLEEVES
Using 4½mm (US7) needles, cast on 48[52,56] sts.
Work 8cm (3in) K1, P1 rib, inc 22 sts evenly across row. 70[74,78] sts.
Change to 5½mm (US9) needles and cont in rib patt as for back, *at the same time* inc 1 st at each end of every foll 6th row until there are 104[108,112] sts.
Cont without shaping until sleeve measures 46[47,48]cm (18[18½,19]in) from top of rib. Cast off.

RIGHT FRONT BORDER
Using 4½mm (US7) needles, cast on 11

sts. Work 15cm (6in) K1, P1 rib, ending with a WS row.
Make buttonhole
1st row Rib 3, cast off 3 sts, rib to end of row.
2nd row Rib to end, casting on 3 sts over those cast off in previous row.
Cont in rib, inc 1 st at end of next and 21 foll 10th rows, *at the same time* make 4 more buttonholes at 11.5[12,12.5]cm (4½[4¾,5]in) intervals.
When border measures same as right front edge, cast off in rib.

LEFT FRONT BORDER
Work as for right front border, reversing shaping and omitting buttonholes.

COLLAR
Using 4½mm (US7) needles, cast on 91 sts.
Work 6cm (2½in) K1, P1 rib.
Change to 5½mm (US9) needles and cont in rib until work measures 13cm (5in) from cast-on edge.
Cast off in rib.

MAKING UP
Join shoulder seams.
Set sleeves in flat matching centre of cast-off edge of sleeve to shoulder seam, and joining last few rows of sleeve to cast-off sts at underarm.
Join side and sleeve seams.
Sew collar to neck edge.
Join on right and left front borders.
Sew on buttons to left front border along join with left front.

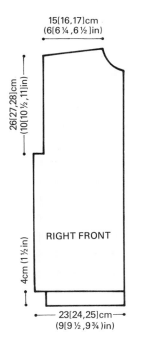

15[16,17]cm (6[6¼,6½]in)
26[27,28]cm (10[10½,11]in)
4cm (1½in)
RIGHT FRONT
23[24,25]cm (9[9½,9¾]in)

16cm (6¼in)
37[38,39]cm (14½[15,15½]in)
½ BACK
51[53,55]cm (20[21,21¾]in)

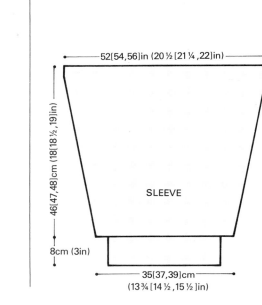

52[54,56]in (20½[21¼,22]in)
46[47,48]cm (18[18½,19]in)
SLEEVE
8cm (3in)
35[37,39]cm (13¾[14½,15½]in)

56

Designed by Filolaine Photograph: Denis Boussard

One-Man Bands

This patterned crew-neck could take many different colour schemes from these clean sharp contrasts to very close tones of greys, browns or even pastel shades.

SIZES
To fit 96[101,106]cm (38[40,42]in) chest

MATERIALS
250[300,350]g (9[11,13]oz) double knitting yarn in main colour (A)
150g (6oz) in each of two contrast colours (B,C)
1 pair each 2¾mm (US2) and 4mm (US6) needles

TENSION
23 sts and 26 rows to 10cm (4in) over patt on 4mm (US6) needles.

FRONT
Using 2¾mm (US2) needles and yarn A, cast on 123[127,131] sts.
Work 7cm (2¾in) K1, P1 rib.
Change to 4mm (US6) needles and commence colour patt from chart, working in st st throughout, as foll:
1st row (RS) K to end in B.
2nd row *P1C, 1B; rep from * to last st, P1C.
These 2 rows set the chart patt.**
Cont in patt as set, rep 1st–94th rows until work measures 51[53,55]cm (20[21,21¾]in) from top of rib, ending with a WS row.
Divide for neck
Next row Patt 53[55,57] sts, turn, leaving rem sts on a spare needle and cont on these sts only for first side of neck.
Keeping chart patt correct, cast off 5 sts at beg of next row and 3 sts at beg of foll alt row.
Work 1 row.
Now dec 1 st at neck edge on next and 6 foll alt rows, ending at armhole edge. 38[40,42] sts.
Shape shoulder
Cast off 9[10,11] sts at beg of next and foll alt row, then 10 sts at beg of next alt row.
Cast off rem 10 sts.
With RS of work facing rejoin yarn to sts on spare needle, cast off 17 sts, patt to end. 53[55,57] sts.
Complete second side of neck to match first side, reversing shaping.

BACK
Work as given for front to **.
Now cont in chart patt as set, rep 1st–94th rows until work measures same as front to shoulder, ending with a WS row.
Shape shoulders
Cast off 9[10,11] sts at beg of next 4 rows, then cast off 10 sts at beg of foll 4 rows.
Leave rem 47 sts on a stitch holder.

SLEEVES
Using 2¾mm (US2) needles and yarn A, cast on 67[71,75] sts.
Work 5cm (2in) K1, P1 rib.
Change to 4mm (US6) needles and work in chart patt as given for front, *at the same time* (inc 1 st at each end of 6th row, then inc 1 st at each end of foll 4th row) 11 times. 111[115,119] sts.
Work straight until sleeve measures 44[45,46]cm (17½[17¾,18]in) from top of rib.
Cast off.

MAKING UP
Join right shoulder seam.
Neckband
Using 2¾mm (US2) needles and yarn A, with RS of work facing, K up 66 sts around front neck, then K across 47 sts from back neck stitch holder. 113 sts.
Work 3cm (1¼in) K1, P1 rib.
Cast off in rib.
Join left shoulder and neckband seam.
Set sleeves in flat, matching centre of cast-off edge to shoulder seam.
Join side and sleeve seams.

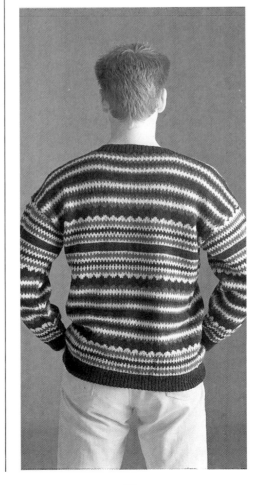

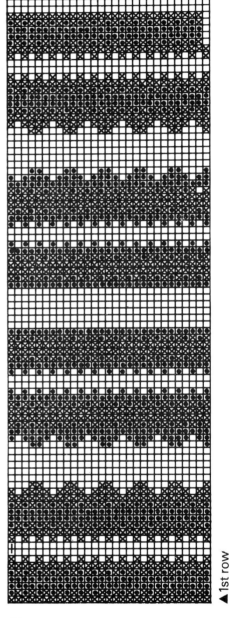

▲ 1st row

☐ = A
☒ = B
⊡ = C

Designed by Sophie Calmat Photograph: Denis Boussard

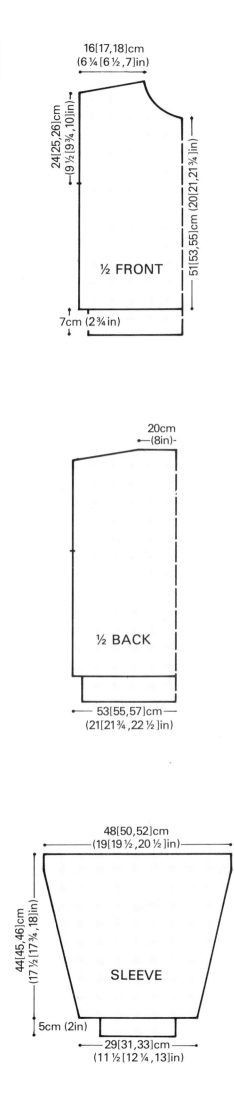

16[17,18]cm
(6 ¼ [6 ½ , 7]in)

24[25,26]cm
(9 ½ [9 ¾ , 10]in)

51[53,55]cm (20[21,21 ¾]in)

½ FRONT

7cm (2 ¾ in)

20cm
(8in)

½ BACK

53[55,57]cm
(21[21 ¾ , 22 ½]in)

48[50,52]cm
(19[19 ½ , 20 ½]in)

44[45,46]cm
(17 ½ [17 ¾ , 18]in)

SLEEVE

5cm (2in)

29[31,33]cm
(11 ½ [12 ¼ , 13]in)

Red Squares

A neat crew-neck sweater with a simple two-colours-a-row pattern. The practical shoulder buttoning makes it painless to put on and off.

AUTUMN
★

SIZES
To fit age 4[6,8] years

MATERIALS
250[300,300]g (9[11,11]oz) four-ply yarn in main colour (A)
50g (2oz) in each of two contrast colours (B and C)
1 pair each 3¾mm (US5) and 4½mm (US7) needles
3 buttons

TENSION
22 sts and 24 rows to 10cm (4in) over st st on 4½mm (US7) needles.

FRONT
Using 3¾mm (US5) needles and yarn A, cast on 74[78,82] sts.
Work 6cm (2½in) K2, P2 rib.
Change to 4½mm (US7) needles and work 2 rows in st st, beg with a K row, inc 1 st at centre of 1st row. 75[79,83] sts.
Cont in st st working from chart as foll:
1st row (RS) K to end in A.
2nd row *P3A, 2B, 1A; rep from * to last 3[1,5] sts, P3A[1A, (3A,2B)].
Cont as set, work 3rd–8th rows from chart, then rep 1st–8th rows until front measures 19[21,23]cm (7½[8¼,9]in) from top of rib, ending with a WS row.
Shape armholes
Cast off 4 sts at beg of next 2 rows, then 2 sts at beg of foll 2 rows. Now dec 1 st at each end of next row. 61[65,69] sts.**
Keeping patt correct, work straight until front measures 7[8,9]cm (2¾[3,3½]in) from beg of armhole shaping, ending with a WS row.
Divide for neck
Next row Patt 26[28,30] sts, turn, leaving rem sts on a spare needle and cont on these sts only for left side of neck.
Cast off 4 st at beg of next row and 2 sts at beg of foll 2 alt rows. Work 1 row. Now dec 1 st at beg of next and foll alt row. 16[18,20] sts.
Now work straight until front measures 12[13,14]cm (4¾[5,5½]in) from beg of armhole shaping, ending at neck edge.
Shape left shoulder
Next row Patt 11[12,13] sts, turn, leaving rem sts on a stitch holder.
Next row Patt to end.
Next row Patt 6 sts, turn, leaving rem sts on a stitch holder.
Next row Patt to end.
Leave rem 6 sts on a stitch holder.
With RS facing rejoin yarn to sts on spare needle, cast off 9 sts, patt to end.
Work straight until front measures 14[15,16]cm (5½[6,6¼]in) from beg of armhole shaping, end at armhole edge.

Shape right shoulder
Cast off 5[6,7] sts at beg of next and foll alt row. Work 1 row.
Cast off rem 6 sts.

BACK
Work as given for front to **.
Keeping patt correct, work straight until back measures 12[13,14]cm (4¾[5, 5½]in) from beg of armhole shaping, ending with a WS row.
Divide for neck
Next row Patt 20[22,24] sts, turn, leaving rem sts on a spare needle and cont on these sts only for right side of neck.
Cast off 4 sts at beg of next row.
Now work straight until back matches front to right shoulder shaping, ending at armhole edge.
Shape right shoulder
Cast off 5[6,7] sts at beg of next and foll alt row. Work 1 row.
Cast off rem 6 sts.
With RS of work facing rejoin yarn to sts on spare needle, cast off 21 sts, patt to end.
Next row Patt to end.
Shape left shoulder
Work as given for left shoulder on front.

SLEEVES
Using 3¾mm (US5) needles and yarn A, cast on 36[40,44] sts.
Work 6cm (2½in) K2, P2 rib.
Change to 4½mm (US7) needles and work 2 rows st st, then work in colour patt from chart as foll:
1st row (RS) K to end in A.
2nd row P0 [(1B,1A), 1A], *3A, 2B, 1A; rep from * to last 0[2,1] sts, K 0[2,1]A.
These 2 rows set the chart patt, cont as set, inc 1 st at each end of 4th and every foll 6th row until there are 52[56,60] sts.
Work straight until sleeve measures approx 22[25,28]cm (8½[9¾,11]in) from top of rib, ending on same patt row as front at armhole.
Shape top
Cast off 3 sts at beg of next 2 rows, then 2 sts at beg of foll 2 rows. Now dec 1 st at each end of next and 7 foll alt rows. Cast off 2 sts at beg of next 2 rows and 4 sts at beg of foll 2 rows.
Cast off rem 14[18,22] sts.

MAKING UP
Button band
Using 3¾mm (US5) needles and yarn A, with RS of work facing K across 16[18,20] sts on stitch holders at left back shoulder.
Work 10 rows K2, P2 rib.
Cast off in rib.

Buttonhole band
Work as given for button band on sts at left front shoulder, making 2 buttonholes on 6th and 7th rows as foll:
1st buttonhole row Rib 4, cast off 2 sts, rib 6 sts including st used to cast off, cast off 2 sts, rib to end.
2nd buttonhole row Rib to end casting on 2 sts over those cast off in previous row.
Join right shoulder seam.
Neckband
Using 3¾mm (US5) needles and yarn A, with RS of work facing, K up 86 sts evenly around neck edge.
Work 2.5cm (1in) K2, P2 rib making buttonhole on 4th and 5th rows as foll:
1st buttonhole row (RS) Rib 2, cast off 2 sts, rib to end.
2nd buttonhole row Rib to end, casting on 2 sts over those cast off in previous row.
Cast off in rib.
Overlap buttonhole band over button band and catch down at shoulder edge.
Join side and sleeve seams.
Set in sleeves. Sew on buttons.

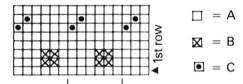

□ = A
⊠ = B
⊡ = C

rep = 6 sts

Designed by Valérie Ribadeau Dumas Photograph: Fouli Elia

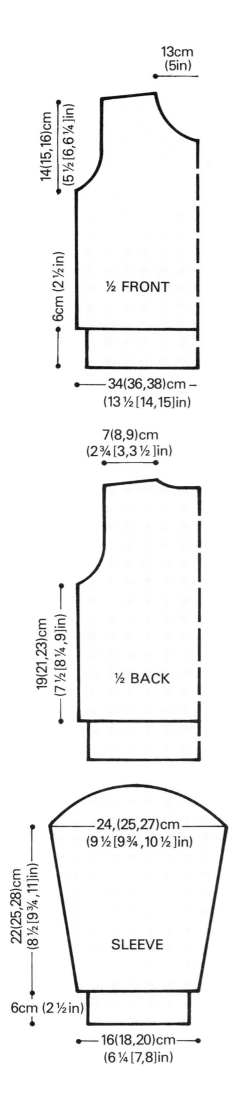

13cm
(5in)

14(15,16)cm
(5½[6,6¼]in)

6cm (2½in)

½ FRONT

— 34(36,38)cm —
(13½[14,15]in)

7(8,9)cm
(2¾[3,3½]in)

19(21,23)cm
(7½[8¼,9]in)

½ BACK

24,(25,27)cm
(9½[9¾,10½]in)

22(25,28)cm
(8½[9¾,11]in)

SLEEVE

6cm (2½in)

— 16(18,20)cm —
(6¼[7,8]in)

Soft Touch

Nothing could be simpler than this sophisticated sweater knitted in silky, soft angora—elegant evening wear for absolute beginners.

SIZES
To fit 81[86,91]cm (32[34,36]in) bust

MATERIALS
325[325,350]g (12[12,13]oz) four-ply yarn
1 pair each 2¾mm (US2) and 3¼mm (US4) needles

TENSION
26 sts and 33 rows to 10cm (4in) over st st on 3¼mm (US4) needles.

FRONT
Using 2¾mm (US2) needles, cast on 124[130,136] sts.
Work 6cm (2½in) K1, P1 rib.
Change to 3¼mm (US4) needles and work in st st until front measures 36 [37,38]cm (14[14½,15]in) from top of rib, ending with a P row.
Shape armholes
Cast off 8 sts at beg of next 2 rows. 108 [114,120] sts.
Now work straight until front of sweater measures 19[20,21]cm (7½[8,8¼]in) from beg of armhole shaping, ending with a P row.
Work 3cm (1¼in) K1, P1 rib for neck border.
Cast off in rib.

BACK
Work as given for front.

SLEEVES
Using 2¾mm (US2) needles, cast on 56[62,68] sts.
Work 5cm (2in) K1, P1 rib.
Change to 3¼mm (US4) needles and work in st st, *at the same time* inc 1 st at each end of every 4th and foll 6th rows alternately until there are 112[118,124] sts.
Now inc 1 st at each end of foll 4th row 114[120,126] sts.
Work straight until sleeve measures 46[47,48]cm (18[18½,19]in) from top of rib.
Cast off rem 114[120,126] sts.

MAKING UP
Darn in ends neatly.
Join shoulder seams to 9[10,11]cm (3½ [4,4½]in) from armhole edge on each side.
Set in sleeves matching the centre of the cast-off edge of the sleeve to the shoulder seam.
Join side and sleeve seams.

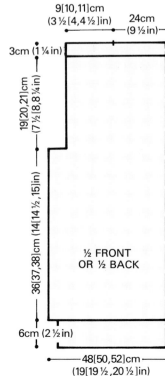

9[10,11]cm (3½[4,4½]in)
24cm (9½in)
3cm (1¼in)
19[20,21]cm (7½[8,8¼]in)
36[37,38]cm (14[14½,15]in)
6cm (2½in)
½ FRONT OR ½ BACK
48[50,52]cm (19[19½,20½]in)

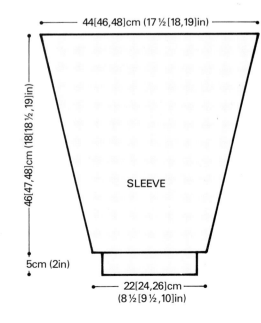

44[46,48]cm (17½[18,19]in)
46[47,48]cm (18[18½,19]in)
SLEEVE
5cm (2in)
22[24,26]cm (8½[9½,10]in)

Designed by Iréna Grégori for Then Photograph: Oliviero Toscani

Shirty

A cosy practical blouson sweater that looks good too. The buttoned front opening makes it easy to pull on and off.

SIZES
To fit age 4[6,8] years

MATERIALS
250[300,350]g (9[11,13]oz) four-ply yarn
1 pair 3mm (US3) and 3¼mm (US4) needles
2 buttons

TENSION
26 sts and 44 rows to 10cm (4in) over moss st on 3¼mm (US4) needles.

FRONT
Using 3mm (US3) needles, cast on 86[92,98] sts.
Work 2cm (¾in) K1, P1 rib.
Change to 3¼mm (US4) needles and work in moss st:
1st row (RS) (K1, P1) to end.
2nd row (P1, K1) to end.
These 2 rows form the moss st patt.
Cont in moss st until work measures 18[20,22]cm (7[8,8½]in) from top of rib, ending with a WS row.**
Divide for neck and shape armhole
Next row Cast off 3 sts, patt 43[46,49] sts including st used to cast off, turn, leaving rem sts on a spare needle and cont on these sts only for first side of neck.
Cont in moss st, work 1 row. Cast off 2 sts at beg of next row and 1 st at beg of foll alt row. 40[43,46] sts.
Work straight until neck opening measures 3cm (1¼in) from beg, ending at neck edge.
Make buttonhole
Next row Patt 3 sts, cast off 3, patt to end.
Next row Patt to end, casting on 3 sts over those cast off in previous row.
Now work straight until work measures 8[9,10]cm (3[3½,4]in) from beg of neck opening, *at the same time* make 2nd buttonhole 4cm (1½in) from 1st buttonhole, and ending at neck edge.
Shape neck
Cast off 9 sts at beg of next row, 4 sts at beg of foll alt row and 3 sts at beg of next alt row. Now cast off 2 sts at beg of foll 2 alt rows. Work 1 row. Dec 1 st at beg of next and 3 foll alt rows. 16[19,22] sts.
Work straight until front measures 13[14,15]cm (5[5½,6]in) from beg of armhole shaping.
Cast off.
With RS facing rejoin yarn to sts on spare needle. Cont in moss st, casting on 6 sts at beg of next row for button band. 46[49,52] sts.
Next row Cast off 3 sts, patt to end.
Complete second side of neck to match first side, reversing shapings and omitting buttonholes.

BACK
Work as given for front to **.
Shape armholes
Cast off 3 sts at beg of next 2 rows and 2 sts at beg of foll 2 rows. Work 1 row.
Dec 1 st at each end of next row.
74[80,86] sts. Now work straight until back measures 4 rows less than front to shoulder, ending with a WS row.
Divide for neck
Next row Patt 23[26,29] sts, turn, leaving rem sts on a spare needle and cont on these sts only for first side of neck.
Cast off 4 sts at beg of next row and 3 sts at beg of foll alt row.
Cast off rem 16[19,22] sts.
With RS facing rejoin yarn to sts on spare needle, cast off 28 sts, patt to end. 23[26,29] sts. Complete to match first side of neck reversing shapings.

SLEEVES
Using 3mm (US3) needles, cast on 34 [40,46] sts. Work 2cm (¾in) K1, P1 rib.
Change to 3¼mm (US4) needles and cont in moss st, inc 1 st at each end of every foll 4th[4th,5th] row until there are 64[72,80] sts.
Now work straight until sleeve measures 23[25,27]cm (9[10,10½]in), ending with a WS row.
Shape top
Cast off 4 sts at beg of next 2 rows, then 3 sts at beg of foll 2 rows. Work 1 row. Dec 1 st at each end of next and 6 foll alt rows. Work 1 row. Cast off 2 sts at beg of next 4 rows, and 3 sts at beg of foll 2 rows, then 5 sts at beg of next 2 rows. 12 [20,28] sts. Cast off.

MAKING UP
Join shoulder seams.
Collar
Using 3mm (US3) needles, with RS of work facing K up 40 sts evenly around right front neck edge beg 1cm (½in) in from edge, 60 sts across back neck and 40 sts around left front neck edge ending 1cm (½in) from edge. 140 sts.
Work 4 rows K1, P1 rib.
Next row Rib to last 25 sts, turn.
Next row Rib to last 25 sts, turn.
Next row Rib to last 40 sts, turn.
Next row Rib to last 40 sts, turn.
Next row Rib to last 55 sts, turn.
Next row Rib to last 55 sts, turn.
Next row Rib to last 70 sts, turn.
Next row Rib across all 140 sts.
Rib 7 more rows. Cast off in rib.
Catch down button band to inside of base of buttonhole band.
Join side and sleeve seams.
Set in sleeves. Sew on buttons.

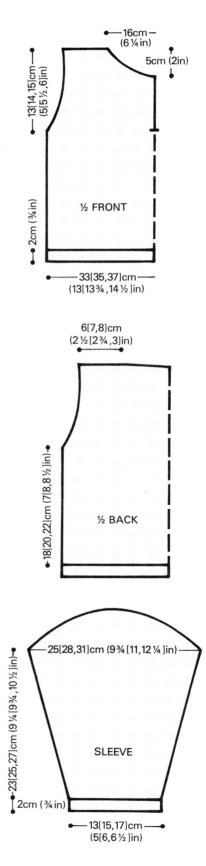

½ FRONT

16cm (6¼in)
5cm (2in)
13[14,15]cm (5[5½,6]in)
2cm (¾in)
33[35,37]cm (13[13¾,14½]in)

6[7,8]cm (2½[2¾,3]in)

½ BACK

18[20,22]cm (7[8,8½]in)

SLEEVE

25[28,31]cm (9¾[11,12¼]in)
23[25,27]cm (9¼[9¾,10½]in)
2cm (¾in)
13[15,17]cm (5[6,6½]in)

Designed by Valérie Ribadeau Dumas Photograph: Sepp

Blazer

**This boxy jacket with shawl collar
could be made up in many
different yarns—here it's in a
smooth chunky pure wool.**

AUTUMN
★

SIZE
To fit up to 96cm (38in) bust

MATERIALS
1100g (40oz) chunky yarn
1 pair each 5mm (US8) and 7mm
(US10½) needles
6 buttons

TENSION
17 sts and 19 rows to 10cm (4in) over rib
patt on 7mm (US10½) needles.

RIGHT FRONT
Using 5mm (US8) needles, cast on 56 sts.
Next row (RS) K6, (K2, P2) to last 2 sts,
K2.
Next row P2 (K2, P2) to last 6 sts, K to
end.
Rep these 2 rows until work measures
6cm (2½in), ending with a WS row, dec 1
st in middle of last row. 55 sts.**
Change to 7mm (US10½) needles and
commence rib patt:
1st row (RS) K6, (K2, P1) to last st, K1.
2nd row (K2, P1) to last 7 sts, K to end.
These 2 rows form rib patt with 6 st-wide
g st border.
Cont in patt as set until work measures
42cm (16½in) from top of K2, P2 rib,
ending with a WS row.
Work collar
Next row K7, rib patt to end.
Next row Work in rib patt to last 7 sts,
K to end.
Next row K8, rib patt to end.
Next row Work in rib patt to last 8 sts,
K to end.
Cont in this way, inc sts worked in g st
on every alt row and dec sts worked in
rib patt, until 22 sts have been worked in
g st and 33 sts have been worked in rib
patt.
Now cont as set until work measures
62cm (24½in) from beg of rib patt,
ending at armhole edge.
Shape collar
Cast off 33 sts at beg of next row. 22 sts.
Work 10cm (4in) g st.
Cast off.

LEFT FRONT
Using 5mm (US8) needles, cast on 56 sts.
1st row (RS) (K2, P2) to last 8 sts, K to
end.
2nd row K6, (P2, K2) to last 2 sts, P2.
Rep these 2 rows until work measures
5cm (2in), ending with a WS row.
Make buttonhole
Next row (K2, P2) to last 8 sts, K4, cast
off 1 st, K to end.
Next row K3, cast on 1 st, K2, (P2, K2)
to last 2 sts, P2.
Now rep 1st–2nd rows until work

measures 6cm (2½in) from cast-on edge,
dec 1 st in middle of last row. 55 sts.
Now complete as for right front from **
to end, reversing g st border and collar
and making 5 more buttonholes spaced
8cm (3in) apart.

BACK
Using 5mm (US8) needles, cast on 90 sts.
Work 6cm (2½in) K2, P2 rib, inc 10 sts
in middle of last row. 100 sts.
Change to 7mm (US10½) needles and
cont in rib patt as foll:
1st row (K2, P1) to last st, K1.
Rep this row until work measures 62cm
(24½in) from beg of rib patt.
Cast off.

RIGHT SLEEVE
Join right shoulder seam.
Using 7mm (US10½) needles, with RS of

work facing K up 79 sts from armhole
edge between two points 23cm (9in) on
each side of shoulder seam.
Work in rib patt as given for back, *at the
same time* dec 1 st at each end of every
foll 6th row until 51 sts rem.
Work straight until sleeve measures
45cm (17¾in) from K up edge.
Change to 5mm (US8) needles and work
6cm (2½in) in K2, P2 rib, dec 1 st in
middle of 1st row.
Cast off in rib.

LEFT SLEEVE
Join left shoulder seam.
Complete as given for right sleeve.

MAKING UP
Join collar seam and sew collar to back
neck edge. Join side and sleeve seams.
Sew on buttons.

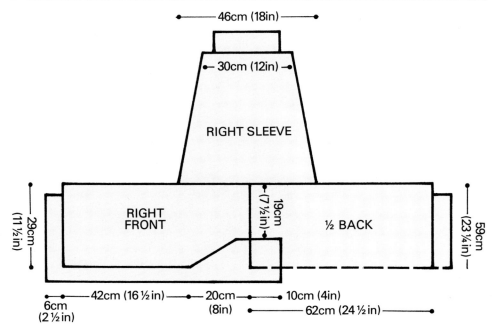

Designed by Soyzic Cornu Photograph: François Pomepui

Classic Cardigan

A beautifully shaped raglan cardigan with carefully crafted saddle shoulders. The shaping is tricky but the stitch is simply stocking stitch.

AUTUMN
★ ★

SIZES
To fit 96[101,106]cm (38[40,42]in) chest

MATERIALS
600[650,700]g (22[23,25]oz) double knitting yarn
1 pair each 3mm (US3) and 4½mm (US7) needles
5 buttons

TENSION
20 sts and 24 rows to 10cm (4in) over st st on 4½mm (US7) needles.

RIGHT FRONT
Using 3mm (US3) needles, cast on 58[60,62] sts.
Work 2.5cm (1in) K1, P1 rib, dec 12 sts evenly across last row. 46[48,50] sts.
Change to 4½mm (US7) needles and work in st st until front measures 35 [36,37]cm (13¾[14,14½]in) from top of rib, ending with a WS row.
Shape neck
Next row K2, K2 tog, patt to end.
Work 5 rows straight.
Next row K2, K2 tog, patt to end. 44[46,48] sts.
Work 1 row.*
Shape raglan armhole
Next row K to last 5 sts, sl 1, K1, psso, K3.
Next row P to end.
Rep last 2 rows once more.
Next row K2, K2 tog, K to last 5 sts, sl 1, K1, psso, K3.
Cont to dec for raglans as set, on 7 foll 6th rows at neck edge and *at the same time*, on 0[1,2] foll alt rows, and then 11 foll 4th rows at armhole edge, ending with a P row. 22[23,24] sts.
Cast off.

LEFT FRONT
Work as given for right front, reversing raglan shaping and working sl 1, K1, psso instead of K2 tog and K2 tog instead of sl 1, K1, psso.

BACK
Using 3mm (US3) needles, cast on 128[132,136] sts.
Work 2.5cm (1in) K1, P1 rib, dec 24 sts evenly across last row of rib. 104[108,112] sts.
Change to 4½mm (US7) needles and work in st st until back measures same as front to *, ending with a WS row.
Shape raglans
****Next row** K3, K2 tog, K to last 5 sts, sl 1, K1, psso, K3.
Work 1 row.**
Rep last 2 rows twice more.
Next row K3, K2 tog, K to last 5 sts,

sl 1, K1, psso, K3.
Work 3 rows.
Rep last 4 rows 11 times more.
Next row K3, K2 tog, K to last 5 sts, sl 1, K1, psso, K3.
Work 1 row.
Next row K2, K3 tog, K to last 5 sts, sl 1, K2 tog, psso, K2.
Work 1 row.
Rep last 2 rows 10[11,12] times more.
Cast off rem 28 sts.

RIGHT SLEEVE
Using 3mm (US3) needles, cast on 46 [48,50] sts.
Work 10cm (4in) K1, P1 rib, dec 6 sts evenly across last row. 40[42,44] sts.
Change to 4½mm (US7) needles and work in st st inc 1 st at each end of 14 foll 6th rows. 68[70,72] sts.
Work straight until sleeve measures 40[41,42]cm (16[16¼,16½]in) from top of rib, ending with a WS row.
Shape raglan
Work as given for back from ** to ** 25[26,27] times. 18 sts.
Shape saddle shoulder
Now work straight until saddle fits across cast-off edge of front, ending with a WS row.
Shape top
Now cast off 6 sts at beg of next and foll alt row.
Work 1 row.
Cast off rem 6 sts.

LEFT SLEEVE
Work as given for right sleeve reversing top shaping.

BUTTON AND BUTTONHOLE BAND
Using 3mm (US3) needles, cast on 10 sts.
Work in K1, P1 rib for 2cm (¾in).
Make buttonhole
1st buttonhole row Rib 4, cast off 2 sts, rib to end.
2nd buttonhole row Rib to end, casting on 2 sts over sts cast off in previous row.
Cont in rib making 4 more buttonholes at 8cm (3in) intervals, until band, when slightly stretched, fits up left front, across sleeve tops and back neck and down right front.
Cast off in rib.

POCKETS (make 2)
Using 4½mm (US7) needles, cast on 30 sts.
Work 12cm (4¾in) st st, then 2cm (¾in) K1, P1 rib. Cast off in rib.

MAKING UP
Join raglan seams.
Join side and sleeve seams.
Join on button and buttonhole band.
Sew on pockets, placing them just above lower rib and 5cm (2in) from side seams.
Sew on pockets.
Sew on buttons.

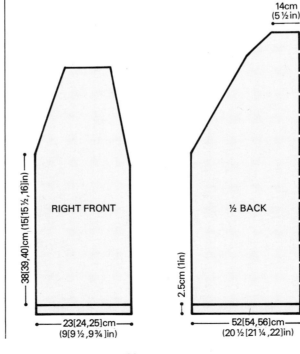
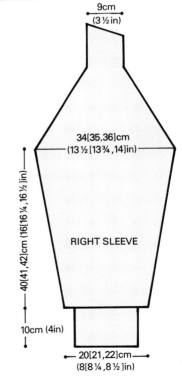

RIGHT FRONT
38[39,40]cm (15[15½,16]in)
23[24,25]cm (9[9½,9¾]in)

½ BACK
14cm (5½in)
68[70,72]cm (26¾[27½,28½]in)
2.5cm (1in)
52[54,56]cm (20½[21¼,22]in)

RIGHT SLEEVE
9cm (3½in)
34[35,36]cm (13½[13¾,14]in)
40[41,42]cm (16[16¼,16½]in)
10cm (4in)
20[21,22]cm (8[8¼,8½]in)

Designed by Valérie Ribadeau Dumas Photograph: Fouli Elia

Gypsy

A colourful cardigan with fronts worked in a simple Fair Isle pattern in six vivid shades. The back is plain, but it and the sleeves could be knitted from the chart if required, though, of course, more would be needed of the contrast colours.

SIZES
To fit age 4[6,8] years

MATERIALS
150[200,250]g (6[8,9]oz) double knitting yarn in main colour (A)
100[125,150]g (4[5,6]oz) in 1st contrast colour (B)
50g (2oz) in each of 4 contrast colours (C,D,E,F)
1 pair each 3mm (US3) and 3¾mm (US5) needles
6 buttons

TENSION
25 sts and 28 rows to 10cm (4in) over patt on 3¾mm (US5) needles.

RIGHT FRONT
Using 3mm (US3) needles and A, cast on 39[42,45] sts.
Work 3cm (1¼in) K1, P1 rib.
Change to 3¾mm (US5) needles and commence colour patt from chart, working in st st throughout, as foll:
1st row (RS) *K1A, 3B; rep from * to last 3[2,1] sts, 1A, 2[1,0]B.
2nd row P1[0,0]B, 2[2,1]A, *1A, 1B, 2A; rep from * to end.
These 2 rows set the chart patt.
Cont in patt, rep 1st–32nd rows, until front measures 25[28,31]cm (9¾[11, 12¼]in) from top of rib, ending with a WS row.
Shape neck
Cast off 10 sts at beg of next row, then 3 sts at beg of foll alt row, then cast off 2 sts at beg of foll 2 alt rows. Work 1 row.
Now dec 1 st at neck edge on next and foll alt row. 20[23,26] sts.
Work straight until front measures 32[35,38]cm (12½[13¾,15]in) from top of rib. Cast off.

LEFT FRONT
Work as given for right front, reversing chart patt and shaping.

BACK
Using 3mm (US3) needles and yarn A, cast on 76[81,86] sts.
Work 3cm (1¼in) K1, P1 rib.
Change to 3¾mm (US5) needles and work in st st, until back matches fronts to cast-off edge.
Cast off.

SLEEVES
Join shoulder seams.
Using 3¾mm (US5) needles and yarn A, with RS of work facing, K up 60[65,70] sts along back and front between two points 12[13,14]cm (4¾[5,5½]in) on either side of shoulder seam.

Work in st st, beg with a P row, dec 1 st at each end of every 7th[8th,8th] row until 40[45,50] sts rem.
Work straight until sleeve measures 29 [31,33]cm (11½[12¼,13]in) from K up row.
Change to 3mm (US3) needles.
Work 3cm (1¼in) K1, P1 rib.
Cast off in rib.

MAKING UP
Join side and sleeve seams.
Neckband
Using 3mm (US3) needles and yarn A, with RS of work facing, K up 25 sts around right front neck, 31 sts across back neck and 25 sts around left front neck. 81 sts.
Work 1cm (½in) K1, P1 rib.
Cast off in rib.
Button band
Using 3mm (US3) needles and yarn A, cast on 11 sts.
Work in K1, P1 rib until band measures 29[32,35]cm (11½[12½,13¾]in) from cast-on edge.
Cast off in rib.
Mark positions for 6 buttons at 1cm (½in) from cast-on edge, 1cm (½in) from cast-off edge, with the rest spaced evenly between.
Buttonhole band
Work as given for button band, making buttonholes opposite button markers as foll:
1st buttonhole row (RS) Rib 5, yfwd, K2 tog, rib to end.
2nd buttonhole row Rib to end.
Sew on button and buttonhole bands.
Sew on buttons.

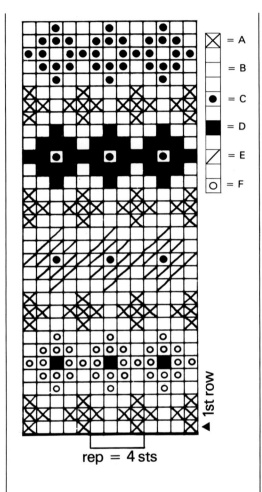

= A
= B
= C
= D
= E
= F

rep = 4 sts

▲ 1st row

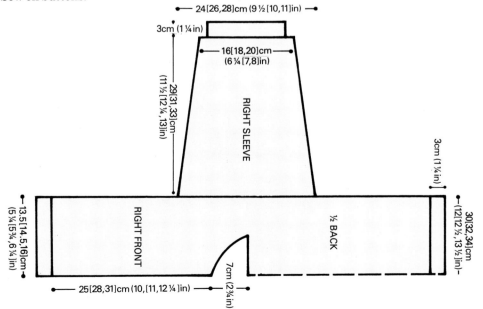

24[26,28]cm (9½[10,11]in)
3cm (1¼in)
16[18,20]cm (6¼[7,8]in)
29[31,33]cm (11½[12¼,13]in)
RIGHT SLEEVE
3cm (1¼in)
13.5[14.5,16]cm (5¼[5¾,6¼]in)
RIGHT FRONT
½ BACK
30[32,34]cm (12[12½,13½]in)
7cm (2¾in)
25[28,31]cm (10,[11,12¼]in)

Designed by Soyzic Cornu Photograph: Christian Maury

Puffed Up

A pretty, fluffy sweater in an interesting ruched pattern made by alternately increasing and decreasing the number of stitches on the needle.

AUTUMN
★ ★

SIZE
To fit up to 91cm (36in) bust

MATERIALS
300g (11oz) double knitting yarn
1 pair each 3mm (US3) and 5mm (US8) needles

TENSION
21 sts and 34 rows to 10cm (4in) over ruched patt on 5mm (US8) needles.

FRONT
Using 3mm (US3) needles, cast on 96 sts.
Work 7cm (2¾in) K2, P2 rib.
Change to 5mm (US8) needles and commence ruched patt as foll:
1st row (RS) *K1, K into front and back of next st; rep from * to end. 144 sts.
2nd–8th rows Work in st st, beg with a P row.
9th row *K1, K2 tog; rep from * to end. 96 sts.
10th–16th rows Work in moss st (see page 121).
These 16 rows form the ruched patt rep.
Cont in patt until work measures approx 28cm (11in) from top of rib, ending with a 10th or 12th patt row.
Shape armholes
Cast off 4 sts at beg of next 2 rows and 3 sts at beg of foll 2 rows. 82 sts.**
Now work straight until front measures approx 40cm (15¾in) from top of rib, ending with a 10th patt row.
Divide for neck
Next row Patt 35 sts, turn, leaving rem sts on a spare needle and cont on these sts only for first side of neck.
Cast off 2 sts at beg of next and foll 3 alt rows. Work 1 row. Now dec 1 st at beg of next and 6 foll alt rows. 20 sts (allow for sts made in patt rows 1–8).
Work straight until front measures

23cm (9in) from beg of armhole shaping.
Cast off.
With RS facing, rejoin yarn to sts on spare needle, cast off 12 sts, patt to end. 35 sts.
Complete to match first side of neck reversing shaping.

BACK
Work as given for front to **.
Now work straight until back matches front to cast-off edge. Cast off.

SLEEVES
Using 3mm (US3) needles, cast on 62 sts.
Work 7cm (2¾in) K2, P2 rib.
Change to 5mm (US8) needles and work in ruched patt as given for front, *at the same time* inc 1 st at each end of every alt 8th and 6th row until there are 76 sts (do not count extra sts made during patt rows 1–8).
Work straight until sleeve measures approx 35cm (13¾in) from top of rib, ending with a 10th patt row.
Shape top
Cast off 5 sts at beg of next 2 rows, then dec 1 st at each end of next and 2 foll alt rows. 60 sts.
Work straight until sleeve measures 39cm (15¼in) from top of rib.
Cast off.

MAKING UP
Join right shoulder seam.
Neckband
Using 3mm (US3) needles, with RS of work facing, K up 110 sts evenly around neck edge.
Work 1cm (½in) K2, P2 rib.
Cast off in rib.
Join left shoulder and neckband seam.
Join side and sleeve seams.
Set in sleeves.

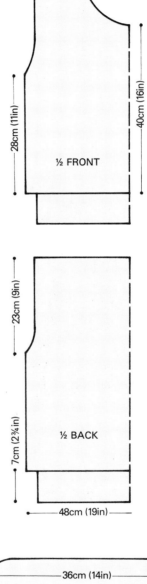

9.5cm (3¾in)   20cm (8in)

28cm (11in)

40cm (16in)

½ FRONT

23cm (9in)

7cm (2¾in)

½ BACK

48cm (19in)

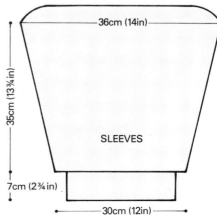

36cm (14in)

35cm (13¾in)

SLEEVES

7cm (2¾in)

30cm (12in)

Designed by Valérie Ribadeau Dumas   Photograph: François Pomepui

Ritzy

Long, slinky lines, a deep scooped neck at back and front and a glittering yarn mixture all add up to a great evening sweater to be flaunted just about anywhere.

SIZES
To fit 81[86,91]cm (32[34,36]in) bust

MATERIALS
300[325,350]g (11[12,13]oz) four-ply yarn
1 pair each 2¾mm (US2) and 3mm (US3) needles

TENSION
29 sts and 35 rows to 10cm (4in) over st st on 3mm (US3) needles.

FRONT
Using 2¾mm (US2) needles, cast on 115[121,127] sts.
Work 6cm (2½in) K1, P1 rib.
Change to 3mm (US3) needles and work in st st, inc 1 st at each end of every foll 10th row until there are 139[145,151] sts.
Work in st st without shaping until front measures 38[39,40]cm (15[15½,16]in) from top of rib, ending with a WS row.
Shape armholes
Cast off 7 sts at beg of next 2 rows, then dec 1 st at each end of foll 3 rows. 119 [125,131] sts.*
Work straight until front measures 41[43,45]cm (16¼[17,17¾]in) from top of rib, ending with a WS row.

**Divide for neck
Next row K54[57,60], turn, leaving rem sts on a spare needle, and cont on these sts only for first side of neck.
Cast off 3 sts at beg of next and foll 4 alt rows, then cast off 2 sts at beg of foll 6 alt rows. Now dec 1 st at neck edge on foll 9 alt rows. 18[21,24] sts.
Work straight until front measures 21 [22,23]cm (8¼[8½,9]in) from beg of armhole shaping, ending at armhole edge.
Cast off.
With RS of work facing, rejoin yarn to sts left on spare needle, cast off 11 sts, K to end of row. 54[57,60] sts.
Complete second side of neck to match first side of neck, reversing all shapings.

BACK
Work as given for front to *.
Work straight until back measures 43 [45,47]cm (17[18,18½]in) from top of rib, ending with a WS row.
Complete as given for front from ** to end.

SLEEVES
Using 2¾mm (US2) needles, cast on 63[69,75] sts.
Work 4cm (1½in) K1, P1 rib.

Change to 3mm (US3) needles and work in st st, inc 1 st at each end of every foll 10th row until there are 83[89,95] sts on needle.
Work straight until sleeve measures 39[40,41]cm (15½[16,16¼]in) from top of rib, ending with a WS row.
Shape sleeve top
Cast off 4 sts at beg of next 2 rows, then 3 sts at beg of foll 4 rows.
Now cast off 2 sts at beg of the next 2[2,4] rows.
Dec 1 st at each end of 16[17,18] foll alt rows.
Now cast off 2 sts at beg of next 2[4,4] rows and then cast off 3 sts at beg of foll 4 rows.
Cast off rem 11 sts.

MAKING UP
Join right shoulder seam.
Neckband
Using 2¾mm (US2) needles, with RS of work facing K up 141 sts around front neck and 119 sts around back neck. 260 sts.
Work 2cm (¾in) K1, P1 rib.
Cast off in rib.
Join left shoulder seam.
Join side and sleeve seams.
Set in sleeves.

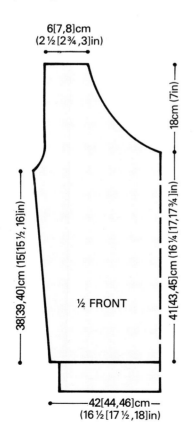

6[7,8]cm (2½[2¾,3]in)

18cm (7in)

38[39,40]cm (15[15½,16]in)

41[43,45]cm (16¼[17,17¾]in)

½ FRONT

42[44,46]cm (16½[17½,18]in)

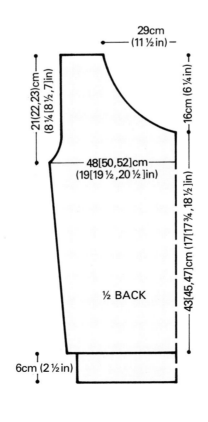

29cm (11½in)

21[22,23]cm (8¼[8½,7]in)

16cm (6¼in)

48[50,52]cm (19[19½,20½]in)

43[45,47]cm (17[17¾,18½]in)

½ BACK

6cm (2½in)

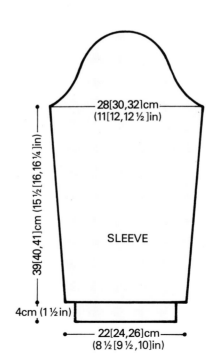

28[30,32]cm (11[12,12½]in)

39[40,41]cm (15½[16,16¼]in)

SLEEVE

4cm (1½in)

22[24,26]cm (8½[9½,10]in)

Designed by Soyzic Cornu Photograph: Christian Maury

Paintbox

Use up all your oddments of brightly coloured yarns in this design. Each small patch of colour will take the merest scrap. Alternatively try lots of skeins of tapestry wools.

SIZES
To fit 81[86,91]cm (32[34,36]in) bust

MATERIALS
500[550,600]g (18[20,22]oz) double knitting yarn in main colour (A)
100g (4oz) in 1st contrast colour (B)
Oddments of assorted colours in a lighter shade (C) and darker shade (D) of each colour
1 pair each 3mm (US3), and 4mm (US6) needles
1 set four double-pointed 3mm (US3) needles

TENSION
21 sts and 30 rows to 10cm (4in) over st st on 4mm (US6) needles.

FRONT
Using 3mm (US3) needles and yarn A, cast on 105[109,113] sts.
Work 5cm (2in) K1, P1 rib.
Change to 4mm (US6) needles and work 12 rows st st, inc 11 sts evenly across 1st row. 116[120,124] sts.
Commence colour patt from chart beg at points X[Y,Z]:
1st row (RS) K1[3,5]A, *2A, 1D, 5C, 13A; rep from * to last 10[12,14] sts, 2A, 1D, 5C, 2[4,6]A.
2nd row P1[3,5]A, 5C, 2D, 2A, *12A, 5C, 2D, 2A; rep from * to last 1[3,5] sts, 1[3,5]A.
These 2 rows set the chart patt.
Cont in patt, staggering the bands of cubes as shown, working 21 rows in A between each band, and using different pairs of lighter and darker shades for each cube as required, until work measures 28[29,30]cm (11[11½,12]in) from the top of the rib, ending with a WS row.
Shape armholes
Cast off 3 sts at beg of next 2 rows then 2 sts at beg of foll 4 rows, then dec 1 st at each end of next and foll 2 alt rows. 96[100,104] sts.**
Work straight until front measures 19[20,21]cm (7½[8,8¼]in) from beg of armhole shaping, ending with a WS row.
Divide for neck
Next row Patt 40[42,44] sts, turn, leaving rem sts on a spare needle and cont on these sts only for first side of neck.
Cast off 3 sts at beg of next row and 2 sts at beg of foll alt row. Now dec 1 st at neck edge on 4 foll alt rows. 31[33,35] sts.
Work straight until front measures 25[26,27]cm (9¾[10,10½]in) from beg of armhole shaping, ending at armhole edge.

Shape shoulder
Cast off 10[11,12] sts at beg of next and foll alt row.
Work 1 row.
Cast off rem 11 sts.
With RS of work facing, rejoin yarn to sts on spare needle, cast off 16 sts, patt to end.
Complete to match first side of neck, reversing shapings.

BACK
Work as given for front to **.
Work straight until back measures same as front to shoulder, ending with a WS row.
Shape shoulders and divide for neck
Next row Cast off 10[11,12] sts, patt 24[25,26] sts including st used to cast off, turn, leaving rem sts on a spare needle and cont on these sts only for first side of neck.
Cast off 3 sts at beg of next row then 10[11,12] sts at beg of foll row.
Work 1 row.
Cast off rem 11 sts.
With RS of work facing, rejoin yarn to sts on spare needle, cast off 28 sts, patt to end.
Next row Cast off 10[11,12] sts, patt to end.
Complete to match first side of neck reversing shapings.

SLEEVES
Using 3mm (US3) needles and yarn A, cast on 35[39,43] sts.
Work 5cm (2in) K1, P1 rib, inc 20[20,18] sts evenly across last row. 55[59,61] sts.
Change to 4mm (US6) needles and work 12 rows st st, inc 1 st at each end of 8th row. 57[61,63] sts.
Commence colour patt from chart beg at points Y[Z,W], *at the same time* inc 1 st at each end of 8th row from previous inc and of every foll 8th row until there are 85[89,91] sts. Now work straight until sleeve measures 42[43,44]cm (16½[17,17½]in) from top of rib.
Shape top
Cast off 4 sts at beg of next 2 rows, 3 sts at beg of foll 2 rows and 2 sts at beg of next 2 rows. Now dec 1 st at each end of next and 16[18,19] foll alt rows. Cast off 2 sts at beg of next 4 rows and 3 sts at beg of next 2 rows. Cast off rem 19 sts.

MAKING UP
Join shoulder seams.
Neckband
Using double-pointed 3mm (US3) needles, with RS of work facing, K up 80 sts evenly around neck edge.
Work 3cm (1¼in) K1, P1 rib in rounds.
Cast off in rib.
Join side and sleeve seams.
Set in sleeves.

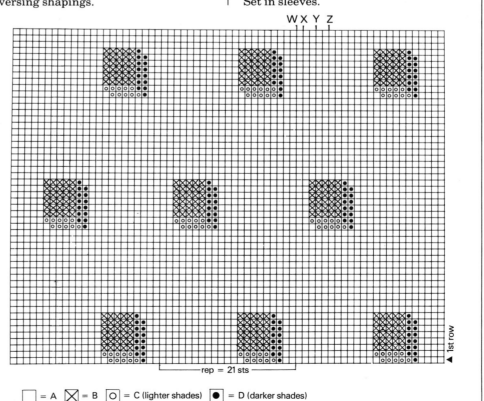

rep = 21 sts

☐ = A   ⊠ = B   ⊡ = C (lighter shades)   ⬤ = D (darker shades)

Designed by Takeshi Yajima Photograph: François Pornepui

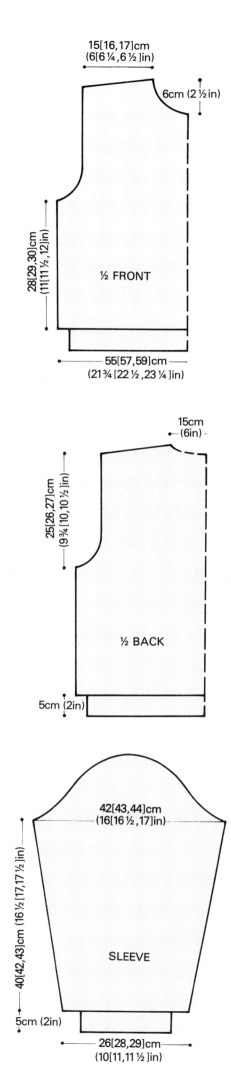

15[16,17]cm
(6[6¼,6½]in)

6cm (2½in)

28[29,30]cm
(11[11½,12]in)

½ FRONT

55[57,59]cm
(21¾[22½,23¼]in)

15cm
(6in)

25[26,27]cm
(9¾[10,10½]in)

½ BACK

5cm (2in)

42[43,44]cm
(16[16½,17]in)

40[42,43]cm (16½[17,17½]in)

SLEEVE

5cm (2in)

26[28,29]cm
(10[11,11½]in)

College Boy

A classic crew-neck, thick-knit sweater with bold asymmetric striping on the sleeves and above the rib.

SIZE
To fit up to 106cm (42in) chest

MATERIALS
500g (18oz) Aran-weight yarn in 1st colour (A)
100g (4oz) in 2nd colour (B)
50g (2oz) in 3rd colour (C)
1 pair each 4mm (US6) and 5mm (US8) needles

TENSION
15 sts and 20 rows to 10cm (4in) over st st on 5mm (US8) needles.

FRONT
Using 4mm (US6) needles and B, cast on 94 sts.
Change to A and work 8cm (3in) K2, P2 rib.
Change to 5mm (US8) needles and work in st st as foll: 1 row in C, 1 row in B.
Cont in st st in A until front measures 35cm (13¾in) from top of rib, ending with a WS row.
Shape armholes
Cast off 4 sts at beg of next 2 rows then 2 sts at beg of foll 2 rows. Now dec 1 st at each end of next and foll alt row. 78 sts.**
Work straight until front measures 17cm (6½in) from beg of armhole shaping, ending with a WS row.
Divide for neck
Next row Patt 35 sts, turn leaving rem sts on a spare needle and cont on these sts only for left side of neck.

Cast off 4 sts at beg of next row and 2 sts at beg of foll 2 alt rows. Work 1 row. Now dec 1 st at neck edge on next and foll 4 alt rows, thus ending at armhole edge. 22 sts.
Shape shoulder
Cast off 8 sts at beg of next row and 7 sts at beg of foll alt row.
Work 1 row. Cast off rem 7 sts.
Rejoin yarn to sts on spare needle, cast off 8 sts, patt to end. 35 sts.
Work 1 row.
Complete right side to match left, reversing shapings.

BACK
Work as given for front to **.
Now work straight until back measures same as front to shoulder, ending with a WS row.
Shape shoulders and divide for neck
Cast off 8 sts at beg of next 2 rows.
Next row Cast off 7 sts, patt 12 sts including st used to cast off, turn, leaving rem sts on a spare needle and cont on these sts only for right side of neck.
Next row Cast off 5 sts, patt to end.
Cast off rem 7 sts.
With RS facing rejoin yarn to sts on spare needle, cast off 24 sts, patt to end.
Cast off 7 sts at beg of next row and 5 sts at beg of foll row.
Cast off rem 7 sts.

RIGHT SLEEVE
Using 4mm (US6) needles and B, cast on

52 sts.
Change to A and work 8cm (3in) K2, P2 rib.
Change to 5mm (US8) needles and work in st st as foll: 1 row in C, 1 row in B.
Cont in st st in A, inc 1 st at each end of 5th and 10 foll 6th rows until there are 76 sts, *at the same time* work in stripe patt as foll: 58 rows in A, 8 rows in B, 8 rows in C, 4 rows in B.
Shape top
Using B, cast off 3 sts at beg of next 2 rows and 2 sts at beg of foll 2 rows. 66 sts.
Now work 8 rows in C and 12 rows in B, *at the same time*, dec 1 st at each end of next and foll 7 alt rows, then cast off 2 sts at beg of next 2 rows and 5 sts at beg of foll 2 rows. 36 sts. Cast off in B.

LEFT SLEEVE
Work as given for right sleeve but in st st stripes above rib as foll: 1 row C, 1 row B, 58 rows in A, 14 rows in B, 14 rows in C, 16 rows in B.

MAKING UP
Join right shoulder seam.
Neckband
Using 4mm (US6) needles and A, with RS facing K up 80 sts evenly around neck edge.
Work 2.5cm (1in) K2, P2 rib.
Cast off in rib in B.
Join left shoulder and neckband seam.
Join side and sleeve seams.
Set in sleeves.

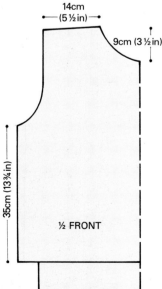

½ FRONT

14cm (5½in)

9cm (3½in)

35cm (13¾in)

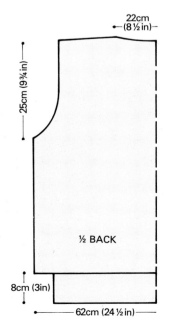

½ BACK

22cm (8½in)

25cm (9¾in)

8cm (3in)

62cm (24½in)

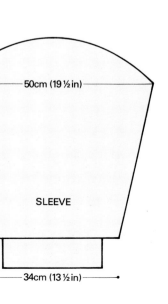

SLEEVE

12cm (4¾in)

50cm (19½in)

40cm (16in)

8cm (3in)

34cm (13½in)

Designed by Valérie Ribadeau Dumas Photograph: Christian Maury

Collage

**A beautiful batwing sleeved
sweater worked in three colours.
Try several versions of this design
using more yarns and working
irregular patches of colour,
changing to a new one as the mood
takes you.**

SIZE
To fit up to 96cm (38in) bust

MATERIALS
250g (9oz) Aran-weight yarn in each of 2
colours (A,B)
150g (6oz) in 3rd colour (C)
1 pair each 5mm (US8) and 6mm (US10)
needles

TENSION
14 sts and 17 rows to 10cm (4in) over
patt on 6mm (US10) needles.

FRONT
Using 5mm (US8) needles and A, cast on
64 sts.
Work 10cm (4in) K1, P1 rib, inc 6 sts
evenly across last row. 70 sts.
Change to 6mm (US10) needles and
commence colour patt from chart (*read
both halves of chart as one chart*),
working in st st throughout and twisting
yarns between colours to avoid a hole, *at
the same time* inc 1 st at each end of 3rd

and every foll alt row until there are 86
sts. Work 1 row.
Shape sleeves
Cast on 2 sts at beg of next 22 rows, then
3 sts at beg of foll 6 rows and 6 sts at beg
of next 2 rows. 160 sts.
Now cast on 7 sts at beg of next 2 rows
and 10 sts at beg of foll 2 rows. 194 sts.**
Now work 20 rows straight, ending with
a WS row.
Divide for neck

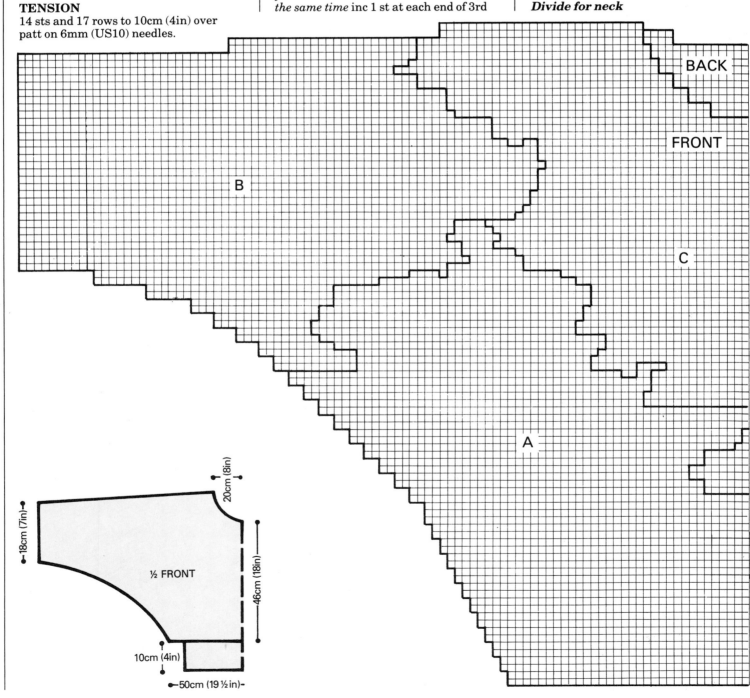

Next row Patt 92 sts, turn, leaving rem sts on a spare needle and cont on these sts only for first side of neck.
Cast off 3 sts at beg of next row, then 2 sts at beg of foll 2 alt rows. Work 1 row.
Now dec 1 st at beg of next row. 83 sts.
Shape shoulder
Next row Cast off 28 sts, patt to end.
Next row Work 2 tog, patt to end.
Next row Cast off 28 sts, patt to end.
Work 1 row. Cast off rem 27 sts.
With RS of work facing rejoin yarn to sts left on spare needle, cast off 10 sts, patt to end. 92 sts.
Complete second side of neck to match first side reversing shapings.

BACK
Work as given for front to **.
Now work straight until back matches front to shoulder, ending with a WS row.
Shape shoulders
Cast off 28 sts at beg of next 2 rows.
Divide for neck
Next row Cast off 28 sts, patt 31 sts including st used to cast off, turn, leaving rem sts on a spare needle and

cont on these sts only for first side of neck.
Cast off 4 sts at beg of next row.
Cast off rem 27 sts.
With RS facing, rejoin yarn to sts on spare needle, cast off 20 sts, patt to end. 59 sts. Cast off 28 sts at beg of next row and 4 sts at beg of foll row. Cast off.

MAKING UP
Join upper right sleeve and shoulder seam.
Neckband
Using 5mm (US8) needles and yarn A, with RS of work facing, K up 71 sts around neck edge.
Work 3cm (1¼in) K1, P1 rib.
Cast off in rib.
Join upper left sleeve, shoulder and neckband seam.
Cuffs
Using 5mm (US8) needles and yarn A, with RS of work facing, K up 31 sts along sleeve end.
Work 7cm (2¾in) K1, P1 rib.
Cast off in rib.
Join side and underarm seams.

For front view of sweater, see next page.

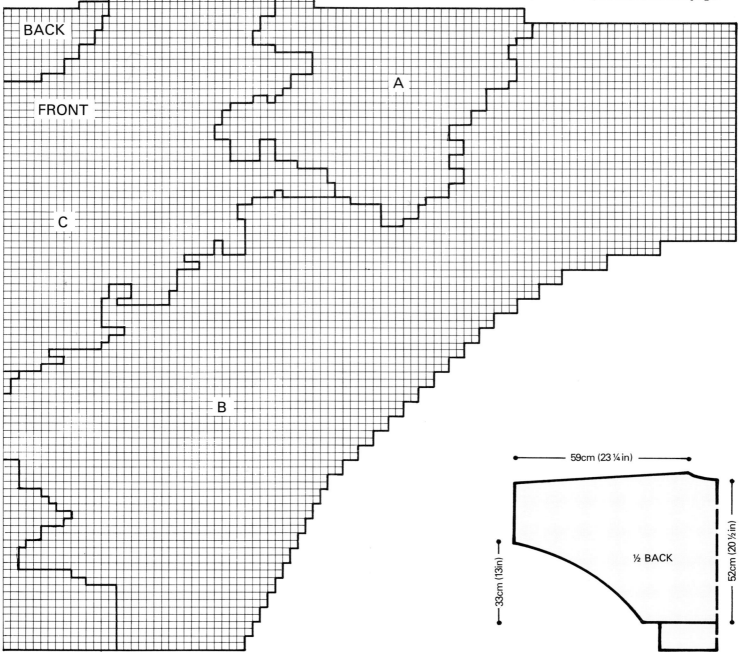

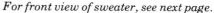

Designed by Brigitte Charoy Photograph: Marie-Laure de Decker

Batwing Jacket

This elegant cabled jacket is worked all in one piece from the hem upwards and the shoulders are joined with a neat crocheted chain.

WINTER
★ ★ ★

SIZE
To fit up to 91cm (36in) bust

MATERIALS
1500g (54oz) Aran-weight yarn
1 pair 4mm (US6) needles
1 4mm (US6) circular needle
1 2.50mm (USC/2) crochet hook
4 buttons
4 press fasteners

TENSION
24 sts and 30 rows to 10cm (4in) over cable patt on 4mm (US6) needles.

RIGHT POCKET LINING
Using 4mm (US6) needles, cast on 40 sts. Work 1cm (½in) st st, ending with a K row. (Inc 1 st at beg of next row, then work 5cm st st, ending with a K row) 3 times. 43 sts.
Inc 1 st at beg of next row, cont in st st until work measures 17cm (6½in), ending with a RS row. 44 sts.
Inc 9 sts evenly across next row. 53 sts. Leave these sts on a spare needle.

LEFT POCKET LINING
Work as given for right pocket lining, reversing shaping.

CABLE PATT
Worked over a multiple of 6 sts, plus 4 extra.
1st row (RS) P3, (K4, P2) to last st, P1.
2nd and every alt row K the P sts and P the K sts of previous row.
3rd row P3, *sl next 2 sts on to cable needle and hold at back of work, K2, then K2 from cable needle, P2; rep from * to last st, P1.
5th row As 1st row.
6th row As 2nd row.
Rep these 6 rows.

TO MAKE (one piece)
Beg at lower edge, using 4mm (US6) circular needle, cast on 224 sts. Work in rows.
Work 3 rows st st, beg with a P row.
P 1 row for foldline.
Work 3 rows st st, beg with a P row.
Commence cable patt as foll:
1st row (RS) P3, *K1, inc 1 in next st, K1, P2; rep from * to last st, P1. 268 sts.
2nd–6th rows As 2nd–6th rows of cable patt.
Cont in cable patt until work measures 5cm (2in) from foldline, ending with a WS row.
Next row Patt 73 sts, K up loop between last st and next st to make 1, P2, make 1, patt 118, make 1, P2, make 1, patt

to end of row. 272 sts.
(Extra sts should occur between 12th and 13th cables and 32nd and 33rd cables.)
Cont in patt (working extra sts in rev st st) until work measures 9cm (3½in) from cast-on edge, ending with a WS row.
Next row Patt 73 sts, make 1, P1, K2, P1, make 1, patt 118 sts, make 1, P1, K2, P1, make 1, patt to end. 276 sts.
Work straight, working extra sts as set, until work measures 13cm (5¼in) from foldline, ending with a WS row.

Next row Patt 73 sts, make 1, P1, K4, P1, make 1, patt 118 sts, make 1, P1, K4, P1, make 1, patt to end. 280 sts.
Cont in patt, working a new cable on 4 extra K sts, until work measures 17cm (6½in) from foldline.
Next row Patt 73 sts, make 1, P2, make 1, patt 130 sts, make 1, P2, make 1, patt to end. 284 sts.
Cont in patt until work measures 21cm (8¼in), ending with a WS row.
Next row Patt 73 sts, make 1, P1, K2, P1, make 1, patt 130 sts, make 1, P1, K2, P1, make 1, patt to end. 288 sts.

Batwing Jacket

Work 1 row.
Place pocket
Next row Patt 25 sts, sl next 53 sts on to a stitch holder, patt across right front pocket lining sts, patt to last 78 sts, sl next 53 sts on to a spare needle and patt across left pocket lining sts, patt to end.

Now work straight until work measures 30cm (12in) from foldline, ending with a WS row.
Divide for back and fronts
Next row Patt 79 sts, turn, leaving rem sts on a spare needle and cont on these sts only for right front and right sleeve section.
Shape sleeve
Cast on 3 sts at beg of next and 31 foll alt rows, *at the same time*, when work measures 32cm (12½in) from cast-on edge, ending with a WS row, shape neck by dec 1 st at beg of next and 18 foll alt rows.

Work straight until front measures 68cm (26¾in) from foldline, ending with a WS row.
Shape shoulder
Next row Patt to last 22 sts, turn.
Next row Patt to end.
Next row Patt to last 44 sts, turn.
Next row Patt to end.
Next row Patt to last 64 sts, turn.
Next row Patt to end.
Next row Patt to last 84 sts, turn.
Next row Patt to end.
Next row Patt to last 104 sts, turn.
Next row Patt to end.
Next row Patt to last 116 sts, turn.
Next row Patt to end.
Next row Patt to last 126 sts, turn.
Next row Patt to end.
Next row Patt to last 134 sts, turn.
Next row Patt to end.
Next row Patt to last 140 sts, turn.
Next row Patt to end.
Next row Patt to last 144 sts, turn.
Leave these sts and rem 12 sts for collar on a spare needle.
With RS of work facing rejoin yarn to sts held on spare needle for back and left front, patt to end.
Shape left front
Next row Patt 79 sts, turn, leaving rem sts on a spare needle for back, and cont on these sts only for left front and sleeve section.
Work left front to match right front reversing all shapings and casting off collar sts.
With WS facing, rejoin yarn to sts held on spare needle for back. 130 sts.
Shape sleeves
Cast on 3 sts at beg of next 64 rows. 322 sts.

Work straight until back measures 68cm (26¾in), ending with a WS row.
Shape shoulders
Shape shoulders by working turning rows as for right front, as foll:
Next 2 rows Patt to last 22 sts, turn.
Next 2 rows Patt to last 44 sts, turn.
Next 2 rows Patt to last 64 sts, turn.
Next 2 rows Patt to last 84 sts, turn.
Next 2 rows Patt to last 104 sts, turn.
Divide for back neck
Next row Patt 48, cast off 18 sts, patt 36 including st used to cast off, turn and leave rem sts on a spare needle.
**Next row Patt to end.
Next row Cast off 5 sts, patt to last 10 sts, turn.
Next row Patt to end.
Next row Cast off 2 sts, patt to last 8 sts, turn.
Next row Patt to end.
Next row Dec 1 st, patt to last 6 sts, turn.
Next row Patt to end.
Next row Leave rem 4 sts on a safety pin.
With WS of work facing, return to sts on spare needle.
Next row Patt to last 12 sts, turn.
Complete to match first side of neck from ** to end.

COLLAR
With WS facing, return to sts on right front for collar. 12 sts.
Cont in patt until collar is long enough to fit around back neck.
Cast off.

POCKET EDGINGS
Using 4mm (US6) needles, with RS of work facing K across 53 sts left on stitch holder at pocket opening, dec 8 sts evenly across row. 45 sts.
Work 3 rows st st, beg with a P row, P 1 row for foldline.
Work 3 rows st st beg with a P row.
Cast off.

MAKING UP
Catch down pocket linings to WS of fronts. Catch down pocket edgings to RS. Join shoulder seams using 2.50mm (USC/2) crochet hook, working single crochet into each corresponding pair of sts from back and front.
Join collar to left front neck edge.
Join on collar to neck edge.
Sleeve edging
Using 4mm (US6) needles, with RS of work facing, K up 56 sts along sleeve edge.
Work 3 rows st st, beg with a P row.
P 1 row for foldline.

Work 3 rows st st, beg with a P row.
Neck and front edging
Using 4mm (US6) circular needle, with RS of work facing, K up 252 sts evenly around edge of right front, across collar, and down left front.
Work 3 rows st st, beg with a P row.
P 1 row for foldline.
Work 3 rows st st, beg with a P row.
Cast off.
Join underarm seams.
Fold all hems on to WS and slipstitch down.
Sew on press fasteners in double-breasted formation, aligning top 2 fasteners with pocket edging and bottom 2 with edge of hem, and overlapping right front over left to edge of left pocket.
Sew buttons on top of fasteners.

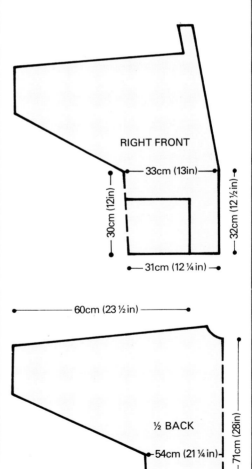

Designed by Anne-Marie Beretta Photograph: François Pomepui

Cowl-Neck Sweater

Knitted almost entirely in stocking stitch with very little shaping, this mohair sweater is an ideal choice for a beginner. The lower edge and cuffs are simply hemmed.

SIZES
To fit 81[86,91]cm (32[34,36]in) bust

MATERIALS
550[600,650]g (20[22,23]oz) chunky yarn
1 pair 6mm (US10) needles

TENSION
15 sts and 18 rows to 10cm (4in) over st st on 6mm (US10) needles.

FRONT
Cast on 72[76,80] sts.
Work 6[7,8]cm (2½[2¾,3]in) st st as foll:
1st row (RS) K to end.
2nd row P to end.
These 2 rows form patt rep.
Cont in st st, inc 1 st at each end of every alt row until there are 96[100, 104] sts on needle.
Shape armholes
Work 26[27,28]cm (10[10½,11]in) straight, ending with a WS row.
Shape shoulders
Cast off 7[8,9] sts at beg of next 4 rows, then 8 sts at beg of foll 2 rows.
Cast off rem 52 sts.

BACK
Work as given for front.

SLEEVES
Cast on 34[38,40] sts.
Work 6cm (2½in) st st.
Cont in st st, *at the same time* (inc 1 st at each end of 4th row, then inc 1 st at each end of foll alt row) 4 times. 78[82,86] sts.
Work straight until sleeve measures 50[51,52]cm (19½[20,20½]in) from cast-on edge.
Cast off.

COLLAR (make 2)
Cast on 54 sts.
Work 2cm (¾in) K1, P1 rib as foll:
1st row (K1, P1) to end.
Rep this row.
Change to st st and work 34cm (13½in) straight.
Cast off loosely.

MAKING UP
Join shoulder seams.
Join both row-end edges of collar pieces neatly so that seam is visible on rev st st side as shown.
Join cast-off edges of the collar to the neck edge.
Set sleeves in flat, matching centre of cast-off edge of sleeve to shoulder seam.
Join side and sleeve seams.
Turn up a 3cm (1¼in) hem on lower edge of back and front, and on sleeve edges and catch down neatly.

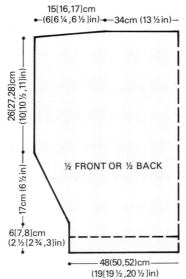

15[16,17]cm
(6[6¼,6½]in)—34cm (13½in)—

26[27,28]cm
(10[10½,11]in)

17cm (6½in)

½ FRONT OR ½ BACK

6[7,8]cm
(2½[2¾,3]in)

— 48(50,52)cm —
(19[19½,20½]in)

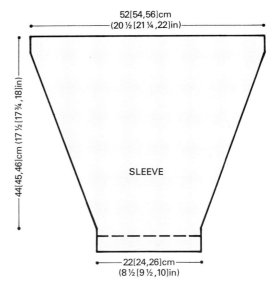

52[54,56]cm
(20½[21¼,22]in)

44[45,46]cm (17½[17¾,18]in)

SLEEVE

—22[24,26]cm—
(8½[9½,10]in)

Designed by Junko Shimada Photograph: Ron Linch

Happy Christmas

A forest of festive Christmas trees are worked into a patterned band on the yoke of a plain stocking stitch cardigan—the perfect Christmas present.

SIZES
To fit age 4[6,8] years

MATERIALS
200[250,300]g (8[9,11]oz) double knitting yarn in main colour (A)
50g (2oz) in each of 2 contrast colours (B,C)
1 pair each 2¾mm (US2) and 3¾mm (US5) needles
7 buttons

TENSION
24 sts and 28 rows to 10cm (4in) over st st on 3¾mm (US5) needles.

RIGHT FRONT
Using 2¾mm (US2) needles and yarn A, cast on 42[44,46] sts.
Work 4cm (1½in) K1, P1 rib.
Change to 3¾mm (US5) needles and work in st st until front measures 23[25,27]cm (9[9¾,10½]in) from top of rib, ending with a WS row.
Commence colour patt from chart, working in st st throughout and weaving contrast colours into back of work, and beg at point W[X,Y] on chart as foll:
1st row (RS) K1[3,5]A, *1B, 5A; rep from * to last 5 sts, 1B, 4A.
2nd row P3A, 2B, *1B, 3A, 2B; rep from * to last 1[3,5] sts, 1B[(1B, 2A), (1B, 3A, 1B)].
Cont in chart patt as set, reading K rows from right to left and P rows from left to right, work 1 row, thus ending at armhole edge.
Shape armhole
Cast off 4 sts at beg of next row and dec 1 st at beg of 5 foll alt rows, *at the same time,* when work measures 3[4,5]cm (1¼[1½,2]in), from beg of armhole shaping, ending at neck edge, shape neck by casting off 5 sts at beg of next row, then 2 sts at beg of foll alt row and 1 st at same edge on foll 9 rows (when chart patt is complete cont in A only). 17[19,21] sts.
Work straight until front measures 14[15,16]cm (5½[6,6¼]in) from beg of armhole shaping.
Cast off.

LEFT FRONT
Work as given for right front, reversing chart patt and all shapings.

BACK
Using 2¾mm (US2) needles and yarn A, cast on 83[87,91] sts.
Work 4cm (1½in) K1, P1 rib.
Change to 3¾mm (US5) needles and work in st st until back measures 23[25,27]cm (9[9¾,10½]in) from top of

rib, ending with a WS row.
Commence colour patt from chart, working in st st throughout, beg at point Y[W,X], work 2 rows.
Shape armholes
Cast off 4 sts at beg of next 2 rows, then dec 1 st at each end of next and 4 foll alt rows. 65[69,73] sts.
Now cont without shaping until the back matches the front to cast-off edge (when chart patt is complete, cont in A only).
Shape shoulders
Cast off 17[19,21] sts at beg of next 2 rows.
Cast off rem 31 sts.

SLEEVES
Using 2¾mm (US2) needles and yarn A, cast on 47[51,55] sts.
Work 4cm (1½in) K1, P1 rib.
Change to 3¾mm (US5) needles and work in st st, inc 1 st at each end of 5 foll 12th rows. 57[61,65] sts.
Work straight until sleeve measures 27[29,31]cm (10½[11½,12¼]in) from top of rib, ending with a WS row.
Commence colour patt from chart beg at point L[M,N], work 2 rows.
Shape top
Cast off 3[4,5] sts at beg of next 2 rows.
Now dec 1 st at each end of next and foll 11[12,13] alt rows, then at each end of next 4 rows, then cast off 2 sts at beg of next 4 rows (when chart patt is complete, cont in A only).
Cast off rem 11 sts.

MAKING UP
Darn in loose ends neatly.
Join shoulder seams.
Neckband
Using 2¾mm (US2) needles and yarn A, with RS of work facing, K up 97 sts evenly around neck edge.
Work 1cm (½in) K1, P1 rib.
Cast off in rib.
Button band
Using 2¾mm (US2) needles and yarn A, cast on 12 sts.
Work in st st until band when slightly stretched measures same as left front opening including neckband—approx 32[34,38]cm (12½[13¾,15]in).
Cast off.
Buttonhole band
Work as given for button band making 7 buttonholes—the first 2cm (¾in) from cast-on edge and the last 2cm (¾in) below neck edge with the rest spaced evenly between as foll:
1st buttonhole row (RS) K2, cast off 2 sts, K4 including st used to cast off, cast off 2 sts, K to end.
2nd buttonhole row P to end, casting on 2 sts over those cast off in previous row.
Fold front bands in half lengthways and sew them on front opening edges.
Neaten buttonholes and top and bottom edges.
Join side and sleeve seams.
Set in sleeves.
Sew on buttons.

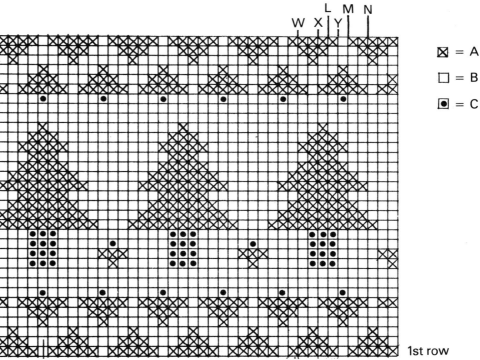

⊠ = A
□ = B
⊡ = C

1st row

Designed by Soyzic Cornu Photograph: Fouli Elia

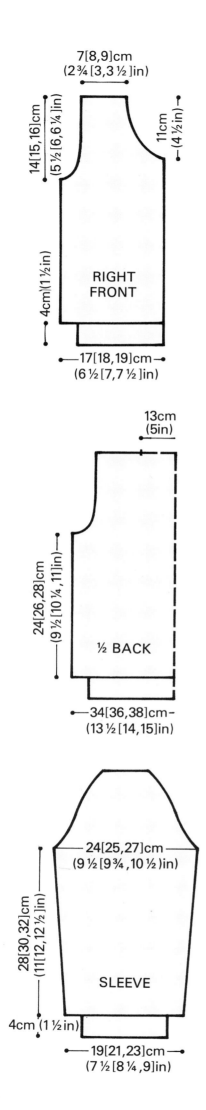

7[8,9]cm
(2¾[3,3½]in)

14[15,16]cm
(5½[6,6¼]in)

11cm
(4½in)

4cm\(1½in)

RIGHT FRONT

17[18,19]cm
(6½[7,7½]in)

13cm
(5in)

24[26,28]cm
(9½[10¼,11]in)

½ BACK

34[36,38]cm
(13½[14,15]in)

24[25,27]cm
(9½[9¾,10½]in)

28[30,32]cm
(11[12,12½]in)

SLEEVE

4cm (1½in)

19[21,23]cm
(7½[8¼,9]in)

Après Ski

After those chilly slopes, thaw out in this elegant polo-neck sweater knitted in bobbly blackberry stitch.

SIZES
To fit 81[86,91]cm (32[34,36]in) bust

MATERIALS
700[750,800]g (25[27,29]oz) four-ply yarn
1 pair each 3mm (US3) and 3¼mm (US4) needles

TENSION
28 sts and 26 rows to 10cm (4in) over blackberry st on 3¼mm (US4) needles.

FRONT
Using 3mm (US3) needles, cast on 138[146,154] sts.
Work 9cm (3½in) K1, P1 rib.
Change to 3¼mm (US4) needles and work in blackberry st as foll:
1st and every alt row (RS) P to end.
2nd row K1,* (K1, P1, K1) all into next st, P3 tog; rep from * to last st, K1.
4th row K1, *P3 tog, (K1, P1, K1) all into next st; rep from * to last st, K1.
These 4 rows form the patt rep.**
Cont in patt until front measures 41[43,45]cm (16¼[17,17¾]in) from top of rib, ending with a WS row.
Divide for neck
Next row Patt 48[52,56] sts, turn, leaving rem sts on a spare needle and cont on these sts only for left side of neck.
Cast off 2 sts at beg of next and foll 3 alt rows, ending at armhole edge. 40[44,48] sts.
Shape shoulder
Cast off 13[14,16] sts at beg of next and foll alt row. 14[16,16] sts.
Work 1 row.
Cast off.
With RS of work facing rejoin yarn to sts on spare needle, cast off 42 sts, patt to end. 48[52,56] sts.

Work 1 row.
Complete to match left side, reversing shapings.

BACK
Work as given for front to **.
Cont in patt until back measures same as front to beg of shoulder shaping, ending with a WS row.
Shape shoulders
Cast off 13[14,16] sts at beg of next 4 rows, and 14[16,16] sts at beg of foll 2 rows.
Cast off rem 58 sts.

SLEEVES
Using 3mm (US3) needles, cast on 56[60,64] sts.
Work 8cm (3in) K1, P1 rib, inc 30[34,38] sts evenly across last row of rib. 86[94,102] sts.
Change to 3¼mm (US4) needles and work in blackberry st as given for front, inc 1 st at each end of every foll 6th row, then foll 5th row alternately, until there are 126[134,142] sts.
Work straight until sleeve measures 46[47,48]cm (18[18½,19]in) from top of rib.
Cast off.

MAKING UP
Join right shoulder seam.
Collar
Using 3mm (US3) needles, with RS of work facing K up 177 sts evenly around neck edge.
Work 24cm (9½in) K1, P1 rib.
Cast off loosely in rib.
Join left shoulder and collar seam, reversing seam to fold on to RS.
Set sleeves in flat matching centre of cast-off edge of sleeve to shoulder seam.
Join side and sleeve seams.

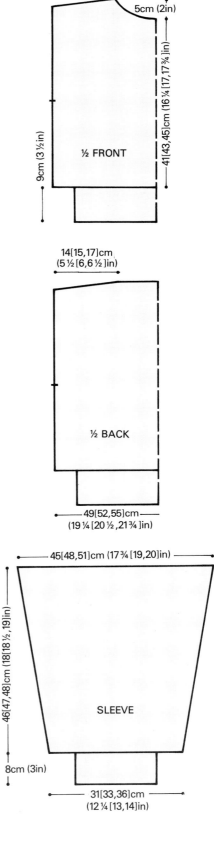

½ FRONT
5cm (2in)
9cm (3½in)
41[43,45]cm (16¼[17,17¾]in)

14[15,17]cm (5½[6,6½]in)

½ BACK

49[52,55]cm (19¼[20½,21¾]in)

45[48,51]cm (17¾[19,20]in)

SLEEVE
46[47,48]cm (18[18½,19]in)
8cm (3in)
31[33,36]cm (12¼[13,14]in)

Designed by Nicole Schmid Photograph: Sepp

Mohair Checks

Glowing orange, ochre and russet on a dark grey background work beautifully together on this warm classic sweater with a deep polo neck.

SIZE
To fit 81–96cm (32–38in) bust

MATERIALS
300g (11oz) Aran-weight yarn in main colour (A)
100g (4oz) each in three contrast colours (B,C,D)
1 pair each 3¾mm (US5) and 5mm (US8) needles
1 set four double-pointed 3¾mm (US5) needles

TENSION
18 sts and 19 rows to 10cm (4in) over patt on 5mm (US8) needles.

FRONT
Using 3¾mm (US5) needles and yarn A, cast on 96 sts.
Work 16cm (6¼in) K2, P2 rib.
P 1 row, inc 6 sts evenly across. 102 sts.
Change to 5mm (US8) needles and commence colour patt from chart, working in st st throughout, as foll:
1st row (RS) *K3A, 3B; rep from * to end.
2nd row *P3B, 3A; rep from * to end.
These 2 rows set the chart patt.
Cont in patt work 3rd–48th row, then rep 1st–48th rows until front measures 26cm (10in) from top of rib, ending with a WS row.
Shape armholes
Dec 1 st at each end of next and 4 foll alt rows. 92 sts.**
Work straight until front measures 22cm (8½in) from beg of armhole shaping, ending with a WS row.
Divide for neck
Next row Patt 33 sts, turn, leaving rem sts on a spare needle and cont on these sts only for first side of neck.
Cast off 3 sts at beg of next and foll 3 alt rows.
Cast off rem 21 sts.
With RS of work facing rejoin yarn to sts on spare needle, cast off 26 sts, patt to end. 33 sts.
Complete second side of neck to match first side reversing shaping.

BACK
Work as given for front to **.
Work straight until back measures same as front to cast-off edge.
Cast off.

SLEEVES
Using 3¾mm (US5) needles and yarn A, cast on 48 sts.
Work 5cm (2in) K2, P2 rib.
P 1 row, inc 9 sts evenly across row.
57 sts.

Change to 5mm (US8) needles and cont in colour patt from chart, beg at 29th chart row as foll:
29th row (RS) K3D, *3A, 3D; rep from * to end.
30th row P3D, *3A, 3D; rep from * to end.
These 2 rows set the chart patt.
Cont in patt, inc and work into patt 1 st at each end of every 4 rows until there are 85 sts.
Work 3 rows.
Cast on 2 sts at beg of next 2 rows.
Work 2 rows.
Now cast on 2 sts at beg of next 2 rows.
93 sts.
Work straight until sleeve measures 42cm (16½in) from top of rib.
Shape top
Dec 1 st at each end of next and foll 5 alt rows. Cast off rem 81 sts.

MAKING UP
Join shoulder seams.
Collar
Using double-pointed 3¾mm (US5) needles and yarn A, with RS of work facing, K up 108 sts evenly around neck edge.
Work 20cm (8in) K2, P2 rib in rounds.
Cast off in rib.
Join side and sleeve seams.
Set in sleeves.
Fold collar on to RS.

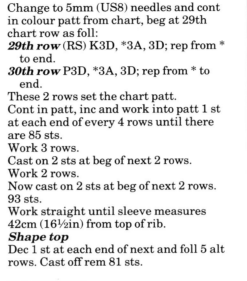

☐ = A
⊡ = B
☒ = C
⊙ = D

1st row

rep = 6 sts

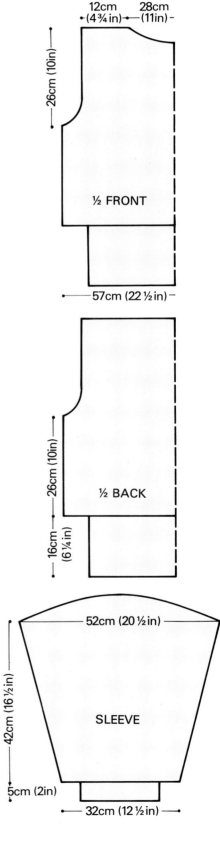

12cm (4¾in) — 28cm (11in)
26cm (10in)
½ FRONT
57cm (22½in)

26cm (10in)
½ BACK
16cm (6¼in)

52cm (20½in)
42cm (16½in)
SLEEVE
5cm (2in)
32cm (12½in)

Designed by Valérie Ribadeau Dumas Photograph: Marie-Laure de Decker

Fisherman's Rib

A simple loose-fitting shape in a chunky rib stitch which has great insulating powers—perfect for breezy afternoons on the water or for frosty winter mornings.

Designed by Valérie Ribadeau Dumas   Photograph: François Pomepui

WINTER
★

SIZE
To fit 81–86cm (32–34in) bust

MATERIALS
950g (34oz) chunky yarn
1 pair each 5mm (US8) and 5½mm (US9) needles

TENSION
16 sts and 30 rows to 10cm (4in) over fisherman's rib patt on 5½mm (US9) needles.

FRONT
Using 5mm (US8) needles, cast on 80 sts.
Work 2cm (¾in) K1, P1 rib, inc 6 sts evenly across last row. 86 sts.
Change to 5½mm (US9) needles and commence fisherman's rib patt:
1st row (RS) K1, *yfwd, sl 1 P-wise, K1; rep from * to last st, K1.
2nd row K1, *P1, K tog sl st and yfwd of previous row; rep from * to last st, K1.
Rep these 2 rows.
Cont in patt until front measures 28cm (11in) from top of rib.
Shape armholes
Cast off 3 sts at beg of next 2 rows and 2 sts at beg of foll 2 rows.
Now dec 1 st at each end of next and foll alt row. 72 sts.*
Work straight until front measures 21cm (8¼in) from beg of armhole shaping.

Divide for neck
Next row Patt 32 sts, turn, leaving rem sts on a spare needle and cont on these sts only for first side of neck.
Cast off 4 sts at beg of next row, then 3 sts at beg of foll alt row and 2 sts at beg of next alt row. Work 1 row. Now dec 1 st at beg of next and foll alt row. 21 sts.
Work 2 rows.
Cast off.
Rejoin yarn to sts on spare needle at centre front, cast off 8 sts, patt to end. 32 sts.
Work 1 row. Now complete to match first side of neck reversing shapings.

BACK
Work as given for front to *.
Work straight in fisherman's rib patt until back measures 23cm (9in) from beg of armhole shaping.
Divide for neck
Next row Patt 30 sts, turn, leaving rem sts on a spare needle and cont on these sts only for first side of neck.
Cast off 5 sts at beg of next row and 4 sts at beg of foll alt row.
Work straight until back matches front to shoulder, ending at armhole edge.
Cast off rem 21 sts.
Rejoin yarn to sts on spare needle at centre back, cast off 12 sts, patt to end of row.
Work 1 row.

Complete to match first side of neck reversing shapings.

SLEEVES
Using 5mm (US8) needles, cast on 50 sts.
Work 2cm (¾in) K1, P1 rib.
Change to 5½mm (US9) needles and cont in fisherman's rib patt, inc 1 st at each end of every foll 6th row until there are 80 sts.
Work straight until sleeve measures 33cm (13in) from top of rib.
Shape top
Cast off 6 sts at beg of next 2 rows and 2 sts at beg of foll 14 rows. Now cast off 3 sts at beg of next 8 rows and 4 sts at beg of foll 2 rows.
Cast off rem 8 sts.

MAKING UP
Join right shoulder seam.
Neckband
Using 5mm (US8) needles, with RS of work facing, K up 88 sts around neck edge.
Work 6cm (2½in) K1, P1 rib, ending with a WS row. P 1 row for foldline. Rib 6cm (2½in).
Cast off loosely in rib.
Join left shoulder and neckband seam.
Fold neckband on to WS of work and catch down.
Join side seams and sleeve seams.
Set in sleeves.

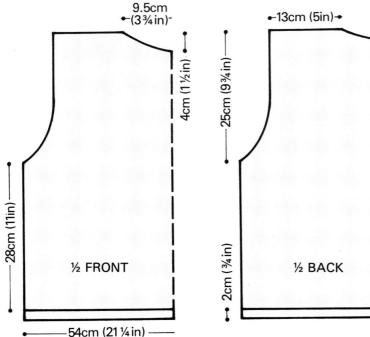

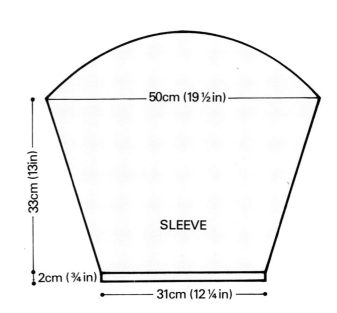

Cherries

A snug crew-neck sweater with a cheerful fruity motif. The back can be either plain, as here, or continued in the cherry pattern.

SIZES
To fit age 4[6,8] years

MATERIALS
150[200,250]g (6[8,9]oz) double knitting yarn in main colour (A)
50g (2oz) each in 1st and 2nd contrast colours (B,C)
1 pair each 3mm (US3) and 4mm (US6) needles
1 button

TENSION
23 sts and 27 rows to 10cm (4in) over st st on 4mm (US6) needles.

FRONT
Using 3mm (US3) needles and yarn A, cast on 69[73,77] sts.
Work 4cm (1½in) K1, P1 rib.
Change to 4mm (US6) needles and work 2 rows in st st, beg with a K row.
Cont in st st, commence colour patt from chart:
1st row (RS) K0[2,4]A, *1A, 2B, 3A, 2B, 2A; rep from * to last 9[11,13] sts, 1A, 2B, 3A, 2B, 1[3,5]A.
2nd row P0[2,4]A, *4B, 1A; rep from * to last 4[6,8] sts, 4B, 0[2,4]A.
These 2 rows establish position of chart.
Cont in patt rep 1st–16th rows on chart, keeping edge sts in A correct, until work measures 15[17,19]cm (6[6½,7½]in) from top of rib, ending with a WS row.
Shape armholes
Cast off 5 sts at beg of next 2 rows. 59 [63,67] sts.
Work straight until front measures 9[10, 11]cm (3½[4,4½]in) from beg of armhole shaping, ending with a WS row.**
Divide for neck
Next row Patt 23[25,27] sts, turn, leaving rem sts on a spare needle, and cont on these sts only for first side of neck.
Cast off 5 sts at beg of next row and 2 sts at beg of foll alt row. Now dec 1 st at beg of 2 foll alt rows. 14[16,18] sts.
Work 2 rows, thus ending at armhole edge.
Cast off.
With RS facing, rejoin yarn to sts on spare needle, cast off 13 sts, patt to end. 23[25,27] sts.
Work 1 row. Complete to match first side reversing shapings.

BACK
Work in A only, shaping as given for front to **.
Divide for back opening
Next row K29[31,33], turn, leaving rem sts on a spare needle, cont on these sts only for first side of opening.

Next row K1, P1, K1, P to end.
Next row K to last 3 sts, P1, K1, P1.
Keeping rib correct as set, work straight until back matches front to shoulder, ending at armhole edge.
Cast off.
With RS of work facing, rejoin yarn to sts on spare needle, cast off 1 st, K to end. 29[31,33] sts.
Next row P to last 3 sts, K1, P1, K1.
Next row P1, K1, P1, K to end.
Keeping rib and patt correct as set, complete second side of opening to match first side.

SLEEVES
Using 3mm (US3) needles and A, cast on 37[41,45] sts.
Work 5cm K1, P1 rib.
Change to 4mm (US6) needles and work 2 rows in st st beg with a K row.
Cont in st st, commence colour patt from chart:
1st row (RS) K0[0,1]B, 0[2,3]A, *2B, 3A; rep from * to last 2[4,6] sts, 2B, 0[2,3]A, 0[0,1]B.
2nd row P0[0,2]B, 0[1,1]A, 0[1,1]B, *3B, 1A, 1B; rep from * to last 2[4,6] sts, 2[3,3]B, 0[1,1]A, 0[0,2]B.
These 2 rows establish the position of the chart.
Cont in patt, *at the same time* inc 1 st at each end of every foll 5th row until there are 61[65,69] sts (work extra sts into cherry patt and when 4th row of triangles in B have been completed, cont in A only).
Work straight until sleeve measures 25[27,29]cm (9¾[10½,11½]in) from top of rib.
Cast off.

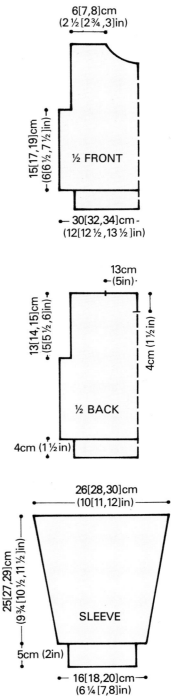

MAKING UP
Join shoulder seams.
Neckband
Using 3mm (US3) needles and yarn A, with RS of work facing K up 89 sts around neck edge.

Work 1cm (½in) K1, P1 rib.
Cast off loosely in rib.
Set in sleeves matching centre of cast-off edge to shoulder seams and last few rows of sleeve to cast-off sts at underarm.
Join side and sleeve seams.
Sew on button to top of neck opening.
Work a button loop to match button on opposite edge.

6[7,8]cm
(2½[2¾,3]in)

15[17,19]cm
(6[6½,7½]in)

½ FRONT

30[32,34]cm
(12[12½,13½]in)

13cm
(5in)

13[14,15]cm
(5[5½,6]in)

4cm (1½in)

½ BACK

4cm (1½in)

26[28,30]cm
(10[11,12]in)

25[27,29]cm
(9¾[10½,11½]in)

SLEEVE

5cm (2in)

16[18,20]cm
(6¼[7,8]in)

☐ = A
☒ = B
⊡ = C

rep = 20 sts

◀ 1st row

Designed by Soyzic Cornu Photograph: François Pompepui

Check Jacket

An elegant jacket patterned in bold checks. Try mixing the textures as well as colours. A tweedy yarn has been teamed with smooth wool here, but mohair or fine bouclé would work just as well.

SIZE
To fit 81–91cm (32–36in) bust

MATERIALS
250g (9oz) double knitting yarn in main colour (A)
150g (6oz) in each of four contrast colours (B,C,D,E)
1 pair each 3mm (US3) and 3¾mm (US5) needles
5 buttons

TENSION
24 sts and 30 rows to 10cm (4in) over patt on 3¾mm (US5) needles.

RIGHT FRONT
Using 3mm (US3) needles and yarn A, cast on 72 sts.
Work 6cm (2½in) K2, P2 rib.
Change to 3¾mm (US5) needles and commence colour patt from chart, working in st st throughout, as foll:
1st row (RS) K8B, *6A, 4B, 6A, 16B; rep from * to end.
2nd row *P16B, 6A, 4B, 6A; rep from * to last 8 sts, 8B.
These 2 rows set the position of the chart.
Cont in patt as set, beg RS rows and ending WS rows 8B on 1st–22nd rows, 8A on 23rd–30th rows, 8E on 31st–34th rows, 8A on 35th–58th rows, 8C on 59th–64th rows and 8A on 65th–74th rows.
Cont in patt, rep 1st–74th chart rows until front measures 33cm (13in) from top of rib, ending with a RS row.
Shape armholes
Cast off 2 sts at beg of next and foll 2 alt rows. 66 sts.
Work straight until front measures 15cm (6in) from beg of armhole shaping, ending with a WS row.
Shape neck
Cast off 6 sts at beg of next row and 4 sts at beg of foll alt row, then cast off 3 sts at beg of next alt row and 2 sts at beg of foll 3 alt rows. Work 1 row. Now dec 1 st at beg of next and foll 4 alt rows. 42 sts.
Work straight until front measures 25cm (10in) from beg of armhole shaping, ending at armhole edge.
Shape shoulder
Cast off 14 sts at beg of next and foll alt row. Work 1 row.
Cast off rem 14 sts.

LEFT FRONT
Work as given for right front, reversing chart patt and all shapings.

BACK
Using 3mm (US3) needles and yarn A,
cast on 144 sts.
Work 6cm (2½in) K2, P2 rib.
Change to 3¾mm (US5) needles and commence colour patt from chart as foll:
1st row (RS) K16B, *6A, 4B, 6A, 16B; rep from * to end.
2nd row *P16B, 6A, 4B, 6A; rep from * to last 16 sts, 16B.
These 2 rows set the position of the chart patt.
Cont in patt as set, beg RS rows and ending WS rows 16B on 1st–22nd rows, 16A on 23rd–30th rows, 16E on 31st–34th rows, 16A on 35th–58th rows, 16C on 59th–64th rows and 16A on 65th–74th rows.
Cont in patt until back measures 33cm (13in) from top of rib, ending with a WS row.
Shape armholes
Cast off 2 sts at beg of next 6 rows. 132 sts.
Now work straight until work measures 25cm (10in) from beg of armhole shaping, ending with a WS row.
Shape shoulders
Cast off 14 sts at beg of next 6 rows.
Leave rem 48 sts on a spare needle.

SLEEVES
Using 3mm (US3) needles and yarn A, cast on 76 sts.
Work 6cm (2½in) K2, P2 rib.
Change to 3¾mm (US5) needles and commence colour patt from chart as foll:
1st row (RS) K9B, *6A, 4B, 6A, 16B; rep from * to last 3 sts, 3A.
2nd row P3A, *16B, 6A, 4B, 6A; rep from * to last 9 sts, 9B.
These two rows set the position of the chart; cont in patt as set, inc 1 st at each end of next and every foll 3rd row until there are 100 sts, then at each end of every foll 4th row until there are 140 sts.
Work straight until sleeve measures 43cm (17in) from top of rib.
Cast off.

BUTTONHOLE BAND
Using 3mm (US3) needles and yarn A, with RS of work facing, K up 118 sts along right front edge.
Work 6 rows K2, P2 rib.
Make buttonholes
Next row (WS) Rib 8, cast off 3 sts, (rib 29 including st used to cast off, cast off 3 sts) 3 times, rib to end.
Next row Rib to end, casting on 3 sts over those cast off in previous row.
Cont in rib until buttonhole band measures 10cm (4in) from K up edge, ending with a RS row.
Make buttonholes over next 2 rows as before.

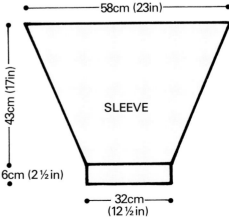

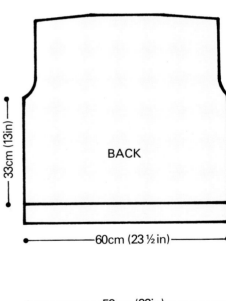

RIGHT FRONT

17cm (6½in)

25cm (10in)

6cm (2½in)

BACK

20cm (8in)

33cm (13in)

60cm (23½in)

SLEEVE

58cm (23in)

43cm (17in)

6cm (2½in)

32cm (12½in)

Designed by Alain Manoukian Photograph: François Pomepui

Rib 6 rows.
Cast off in rib.

BUTTON BAND
Work as given for buttonhole band,
omitting buttonholes.

MAKING UP
Join shoulder seams.
Fold button and buttonhole bands in half
on to WS and catch down.
Neaten buttonholes.
Neckband
Using 3mm (US3) needles and yarn A,
with RS of work facing, K up 41 sts
around right front neck, K across 48 sts
across back neck, then K up 41 sts
around left front neck. 130 sts.
Work 6 rows K2, P2 rib.
Make buttonhole
Next row Rib to last 11 sts, cast off 3 sts,
   rib to end.
Next row Rib to end, casting on 3 sts
   over those cast off in previous row.
Cont in rib until neckband measures
9cm (3¾in) from K up row, ending with
a RS row.
Make buttonhole on next 2 rows as
before.
Rib 6 rows.
Cast off in rib.
Fold neckband in half on to WS and
catch down.
Neaten buttonhole.
Join side and sleeve seams.
Set in sleeves.
Sew on buttons.

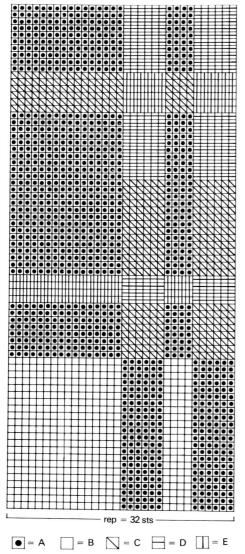

└── rep = 32 sts ──┘

● = A   ☐ = B   ◩ = C   ⊟ = D   ▯ = E

Fast and Loose

**This huge, roomy, ribbed sweater
with a narrow stand-up collar can
be knitted up in next to no time.**

SIZE
To fit 81–96cm (32–38in) bust

MATERIALS
650g (23oz) Aran-weight yarn
1 pair each 5mm (US8) and 6mm (US10)
needles

TENSION
16 sts and 24 rows to 10cm (4in) over rib
patt on 6mm (US10) needles.

FRONT
Using 5mm (US8) needles, cast on 101
sts.
1st row P2, *K1, P2; rep from * to end.
2nd row K2, *P1, K2; rep from * to end.
Rep these 2 rows until work measures
8cm (3in), ending with a 1st row.
Change to 6mm (US10) needles and
commence rib patt:
1st row (WS) K to end.
2nd row P2, *K next st in row below,
P2; rep from * to end.
These 2 rows form the patt rep.
Cont in rib patt until work measures
35cm (13¾in) from top of P2, K1 rib,
ending with a WS row.
Shape armholes
Cast off 4 sts at beg of next 2 rows and 3
sts at beg of foll 2 rows. Cast off 2 sts at
beg of next 2 rows, then dec 1 st at each
end of next row. 81 sts.**
Work straight until front measures
52cm (6½in) from beg of armhole
shaping, ending with a WS row.
Divide for neck
Next row Patt 34 sts, turn, leaving rem
sts on a spare needle and cont on these
sts only for first side of neck.
Cast off 4 sts at beg of next row, 3 sts at
beg of foll alt row and 2 sts at beg of next
alt row. Dec 1 st at beg of foll alt row.
24 sts.
Work straight until front measures
25cm (10in) from beg of armhole
shaping.
Cast off.
With RS facing rejoin yarn to sts on
spare needle, cast off 13 sts, patt to end.
34 sts.
Complete to match first side of neck
reversing shaping.

BACK
Work as given for front to **.
Now work straight until back measures
same as front to cast-off edge.
Cast off.

SLEEVES
Using 5mm (US8) needles, cast on 42 sts.
Work 8cm (3in) P2, K1 rib, inc 11 sts
evenly across last row. 53 sts.

Change to 6mm (US10) needles and
work in rib patt as for front, *at the same
time* inc 1 st at each end of every foll 6th
row until there are 83 sts.
Now work straight until sleeve
measures 40cm (16in) from top of P2, K1
rib, ending with a WS row.
Shape top
Dec 1 st at each end of next row. Work 1
row. Cast off 2 sts at beg of next row, 3
sts at beg of foll 2 rows and 4 sts at beg of
next 2 rows.
Cast off rem 63 sts.

MAKING UP
Join right shoulder seam.
Neckband
Using 5mm (US8) needles, with RS of
work facing K up 87 sts around neck
edge.
Work 6cm (2½in) P2, K1 rib, ending
with a WS row.
P 1 row for foldline.
Work 6cm (2½in) P2, K1 rib.
Cast off in rib.
Join left shoulder and neckband seam.
Fold neckband on to WS and catch down.
Join side and sleeve seams.
Set in sleeves.

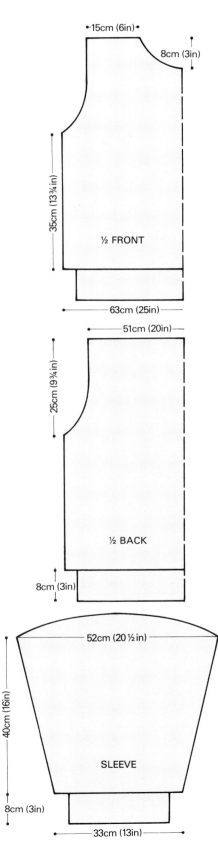

• 15cm (6in) •

8cm (3in)

35cm (13¾in)

½ FRONT

63cm (25in)

51cm (20in)

25cm (9¾in)

½ BACK

8cm (3in)

52cm (20½in)

40cm (16in)

SLEEVE

8cm (3in)

33cm (13in)

Designed by Valérie Ribadeau Dumas Photograph: Christian Maury

Plaid

A snug cardigan with a tartan flavour. The back can be plain, as here, or worked in the same pattern as the fronts.

SIZE
To fit up to 91cm (36in) bust

MATERIALS
500g (18oz) double knitting yarn in main colour (A)
150g (6oz) in 1st contrast colour (B)
50g (2oz) in 2nd contrast colour (C)
1 pair each 3mm (US3) and 4mm (US6) needles
5 buttons

TENSION
24 sts and 30 rows to 10cm (4in) over patt on 4mm (US6) needles.

POCKET LININGS (make 2)
Using 4mm (US6) needles and yarn A, cast on 36 sts.
Work 12cm (4¾in) st st, ending with a WS row.
Leave these sts on a stitch holder.

RIGHT FRONT
Using 3mm (US3) needles and yarn A, cast on 70 sts.
Work 6cm (2½in) K1, P1 rib; dec 5 sts evenly across last row. 65 sts.
Change to 4mm (US6) needles and commence colour patt from chart as foll:
1st row (RS) *K(1A, 1B) 3 times, 6B; rep from * to last 5 sts, (1A, 1B) twice, 1A.
2nd row P(1A, 1B) twice, 1A, *7B, (1A, 1B) twice, 1A.
These 2 rows set the chart patt.
Cont in patt, rep 1st–16th rows, until front measures 12cm (4¾in) from top of rib, ending with a WS row.
Place pocket
Next row Patt 18 sts, sl next 36 sts on LH needle on to a stitch holder and patt across 36 sts left on stitch holder for pocket lining, patt to end. 65 sts.
Cont in patt until front measures 30cm (12in) from top of rib, ending with a WS row.
Shape neck
Keeping patt correct, dec 1 st at beg of next and foll 4th row, (then 1 st at same edge on 3rd and foll 4th row) 12 times, *at the same time*, when work measures 37cm (14¾in) from top of rib, ending at armhole edge, shape armhole by casting off 3 sts at beg of next row and 2 sts at beg of foll alt row, then dec 1st at armhole edge on 4 foll 6th rows. 30 sts.
Work straight until front measures 27cm (10½in) from beg of armhole shaping. Cast off.

LEFT FRONT
Work as given for fright front, working between left front markers on chart and reversing shapings and pocket placing.

BACK
Using 3mm (US3) needles and yarn A, cast on 126 sts.
Work 6cm (2½in) K1, P1 rib, dec 12 sts evenly across last row. 114 sts.
Change to 4mm (US6) needles and work in st st until back measures same as fronts to beg of armhole shaping, ending with a WS row.
Shape armholes
Cast off 3 sts at beg of next 2 rows and 2 sts at beg of foll 2 rows. 104 sts.
Now dec 1 st at each end of 4 foll 6th rows. 96 sts. Work straight until back measures 27cm (10½in) from beg of armhole shaping. Cast off.

SLEEVES
Using 3mm (US3) needles and A, cast on 68 sts. Work 6cm (2½in) K1, P1 rib.
Change to 4mm (US6) needles and work in st st, inc 1 st at each end of every 4th row until there are 114 sts.
Work straight until sleeve measures 34cm (13½in) from top of rib.
Shape top
Dec 1 st at each end of next and foll 2 alt rows, then cast off 2 sts at beg of next 2 rows. Work 1 row. Cast off 3 sts at beg of next 2 rows, 4 sts at beg of foll 2 rows and 5 sts at beg of next 2 rows, then 6 sts at beg of next 10 rows. Cast off rem 20 sts.

MAKING UP
Join shoulder seams.
Front band
Using 3mm (US3) needles and A, cast on 12 sts. Work 2cm (¾in) K1, P1 rib.
Make buttonhole
1st row (RS) Rib 5, cast off 2, rib to end.
2nd row Rib to end, casting on 2 sts over those cast off in previous row.
Cont in rib, making 4 more buttonholes at 7cm (2¾in) intervals until front band, when slightly stretched, fits up right front, across back neck and down left front. Cast off.
Join side and sleeve seams. Set in sleeves. Sew on front band. Sew on buttons.

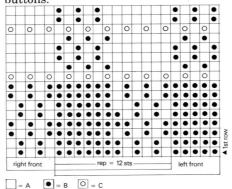

right front   rep = 12 sts   left front

▲ 1st row

□ = A   ● = B   ○ = C

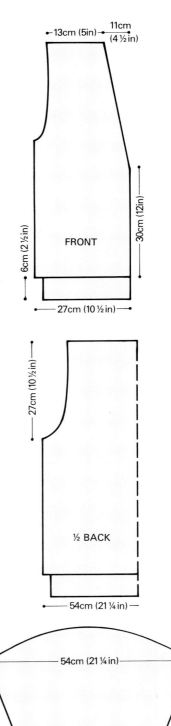

←13cm (5in)→ 11cm (4½in)

6cm (2½in)

FRONT

30cm (12in)

←27cm (10½in)→

27cm (10½in)

½ BACK

←54cm (21¼in)→

54cm (21¼in)

34cm (13½in)

SLEEVE

6cm (2½in)

←31cm (12¼in)→

Designed by Valérie Ribadeau Dumas Photograph: Christian Maury

Popcorn Sweater

Panels of popcorn stitches, Irish moss stitch and intricate interlaced cables are the features of this Aran-style sweater.

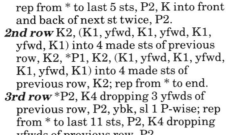

SIZE
To fit up to 101cm (40in) bust

MATERIALS
900g (32oz) Aran-weight yarn
1 pair each 5mm (US8) and 5½mm (US9) needles

TENSION
18 sts and 20 rows to 10cm (4in) over Irish moss st on 5½mm (US9) needles.

SPECIAL ABBREVIATIONS
C4B (cable 4 back)—sl next 2 sts on to cable needle and hold at back of work, K2, then K2 from cable needle.
C4F (cable 4 front)—sl next 2 sts on to cable needle and hold at front of work, K2, then K2 from cable needle.
Tw3L (twist 3 left)—sl next 2 sts on to cable needle and hold at front of work, P1, then K2 from cable needle.
Tw3R (twist 3 right)—sl next st on to cable needle and hold at back of work, K2, then P1 from cable needle.

IRISH MOSS ST
Worked over an odd number of sts.
1st row (RS) (K1, P1) to last st, K1.
2nd row (P1, K1) to last st, P1.
3rd row As 2nd row.
4th row As 1st row.
Rep these 4 rows.

PANEL PATT 1
Worked over 2 sts.
1st row (RS) K 2nd st on LH needle, then K 1st st, dropping both sts off needle at the same time.
2nd row P to end.
Rep these 2 rows.

PANEL PATT 2
Worked over 16 sts.
1st row (RS) K2, P4, K4, P4, K2.
2nd and every alt row K the P sts and P the K sts of previous row.
3rd row K2, P4, C4B, P4, K2.
5th row (Tw3L, P2, Tw3R) twice.
7th row (P1, Tw3L, Tw3R, P1) twice.
9th row P2, C4B, P4, C4F, P2.
11th row K the P sts and P the K sts of previous row.
13th row As 9th row.
15th row (P1, Tw3R, Tw3L, P1) twice.
17th row (Tw3R, P2, Tw3L) twice.
19th row As 3rd row.
20th row As 2nd row.
Rep these 20 rows.

PANEL PATT 3
Worked over 23 sts.
1st row (RS) *P2, K into front and back of next st twice, P2, ybk, sl 1 P-wise; rep from * to last 5 sts, P2, K into front and back of next st twice, P2.
2nd row K2, (K1, yfwd, K1, yfwd, K1, yfwd, K1) into 4 made sts of previous row, K2, *P1, K2, (K1, yfwd, K1, yfwd, K1, yfwd, K1) into 4 made sts of previous row, K2; rep from * to end.
3rd row *P2, K4 dropping 3 yfwds of previous row, P2, ybk, sl 1 P-wise; rep from * to last 11 sts, P2, K4 dropping yfwds of previous row, P2.
4th row As 2nd row.
5th row As 3rd row.
6th row K2, K4 tog, K2, *P1, K2, K4 tog, K2; rep from * to end.
7th row *P2, ybk, sl 1 P-wise, P2, K into front and back of next st twice; rep from * to last 5 sts, P2, ybk, sl 1 P-wise, P2.
8th row K2, P1, K2, *(K1, yfwd, K1, yfwd, K1, yfwd, K1) into 4 made sts of previous row, K2, P1, K2; rep from * to end.
9th row *P2, ybk, sl 1 P-wise, P2, K4 dropping yfwds of previous row; rep from * to last 5 sts, P2, ybk, sl 1 P-wise, P2.
10th row As 8th row.
11th row As 9th row.
12th row K2, P1, K2, *K4 tog, K2, P1, K2; rep from * to end.
Rep these 12 rows.

FRONT
Using 5mm (US8) needles, cast on 95 sts.
Work 7cm (2¾in) K1, P1 rib, inc 14 sts evenly across last row. 109 sts.
Change to 5½mm (US9) needles and commence patt as foll:
1st row (RS) Work 15 sts Irish moss st, P1, 1st row panel patt 1, P3, 1st row panel patt 2, P3, 1st row panel patt 1, P1, 1st row panel patt 3, P1, 1st row panel patt 1, P3, 1st row panel patt 2, P3, 1st row panel patt 1, P1, 15 sts Irish moss st.
2nd row Work 15 sts Irish moss st, K1, 2nd row panel patt 1, K3, 2nd row panel patt 2, K3, 2nd row panel patt 1, K1, 2nd row panel patt 3, K1, 2nd row panel patt 1, K3, 2nd row panel patt 2, K3, 2nd row panel patt 1, K1, 15 sts Irish moss st.
These 2 rows set position of panel patts.
Cont as set until work measures 31cm (12¼in) from top of rib, ending with a WS row.
Shape armholes
Cast off 3 sts at beg of next 4 rows, then 2 sts at beg of foll 4 rows. Now dec 1 st at each end of next and foll alt row. 85 sts.**
Work straight until front measures 17cm (6½in) from beg of armhole

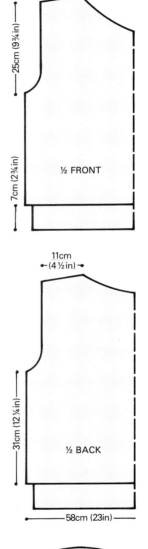

Designed by Aline Fayet Photograph: François Pomepui

shaping, ending with a WS row.

Divide for neck

Next row Patt 24 sts, turn, leaving rem sts on a spare needle and cont on these sts only for left side of neck.
Cast off 3 sts at beg of next row, then dec 1 st at neck edge on 3 foll alt rows.
Work straight until front measures 25cm (10in) from beg of armhole shaping, ending at armhole edge.

Shape shoulder

Cast off 6 sts at beg of next and foll alt row. Work 1 row.
Cast off rem 6 sts.
With RS of work facing rejoin yarn to sts on spare needle, cast off 37 sts, patt to end.
Complete to match first side of neck, reversing all shapings.

BACK

Work as given for front to **.
Now work straight until back measures 6 rows less than front to shoulder, ending with a WS row.

Divide for neck

Next row Patt 22 sts, turn, leaving rem sts on a spare needle and cont on these sts only for first side of neck.
Cast off 3 sts at beg of next row and dec 1 st at beg of foll alt row. Work 2 rows straight, ending at armhole edge.

Shape shoulder

Cast off 6 sts at beg of next and foll alt row. Work 1 row.
Cast off rem 6 sts.
With RS of work facing rejoin yarn to sts on spare needle, cast off 41 sts, patt to end. 22 sts.
Complete to match first side of neck reversing all shapings.

SLEEVES

Using 5mm (US8) needles, cast on 44 sts.
Work 7cm (2¾in) K1, P1 rib, inc 18 sts evenly across last row. 62 sts.
Change to 5½mm (US9) needles and commence panel patts as foll:

1st row (RS) Work 17 sts Irish moss st, 1st row panel patt 1, P4, 1st row panel patt 2, P4, 1st row panel patt 1, 17 sts Irish moss st.

2nd row Work 17 sts Irish moss st, 2nd row panel patt 1, K4, 2nd row panel patt 2, K4, 2nd row panel patt 1, 17 sts Irish moss st.

Cont as set inc 1 st at each end of foll 8th row and of 3 foll 10th rows, then of 5 foll 8th rows. 70 sts.
Work straight until sleeve measures 42cm (16½in) from top of rib.

Shape top

(Cast off 2 sts at beg of next 2 rows then dec 1 st at each end of next and foll alt row) 3 times. Now cast off 2 sts at beg of next 2 rows and 3 sts at beg of foll 4 rows, then 4 sts at beg of next 4 rows.
Cast off rem 24 sts.

MAKING UP

Join right shoulder seam.

Neckband

Using 5mm (US8) needles, with RS of work facing, K up 125 sts evenly around neck edge.
Work 4cm (1½in) K1, P1 rib.
Cast off in rib.
Join left shoulder and neckband seam.
Join side and sleeve seams.
Set in sleeves.

Leaf Sweater

Knitted in softest alpaca yarn, this crew-neck sweater is beautifully patterned with frosty leaves across the yoke and upper sleeves. Both neckband, cuffs and lower rib are double for extra warmth.

WINTER
★ ★ ★

SIZES
To fit 81[86,91]cm (32[34,36]in) bust

MATERIALS
300[350,400]g (11[13,15]oz) four-ply yarn in main colour (A)
100g (4oz) in contrast colour (B)
1 pair each 2¼mm (US1) and 3mm (US3) needles
1 set four double-pointed 2¼mm (US1) needles

TENSION
29 sts and 36 rows to 10cm (4in) over st st on 3mm (US3) needles.

FRONT
Using 2¼mm (US1) needles and yarn B, cast on 137[143,149] sts.
Work in K3, P1 rib as foll:
1st row (RS) K0[1,0], P1, *K3, P1; rep from * to last 0[1,0] sts, K0[1,0].
2nd row K the P sts and P the K sts of previous row.
Rep these 2 rows.
Cont in rib until work measures 12cm (4¾in) from cast-on edge, ending with a 2nd row.
Change to 3mm (US3) needles and commence colour patt from chart 1, working in st st throughout, as foll:
1st–4th rows Work in st st in B only.
5th row K1[2,1]B, *K1B, 1A, 2B; rep from * to last 0[1,0] sts, K0[1,0]B.
6th row P0[1,0]B, *2B, 1A, 1B; rep from * to last 1[2,1] sts, P to end in B.
These 6 rows set the chart patt.
Cont in patt, work 7th–11th rows from chart.
Now cont in st st in A only until work measures 37[38,39]cm (14½[15,15½]in) from top of rib, ending with a WS row.
Commence patt from chart 2, work 2 rows.**
Shape armholes
Keeping chart patt correct, cast off 1[2,3] sts at beg of next 2 rows, then dec 1 st at each end of next and every foll alt row until 63 sts rem, ending with a WS row (when chart patt is complete, cont in B only).
Divide for neck
Next row Patt to end, casting off centre 13 sts.
Next row Patt to neck edge, turn, leaving rem sts on a spare needle and cont on these sts only for first side of neck.
Keeping armhole decs correct as set, cast off 3 sts at beg of next and foll alt row, then 2 sts at beg of foll 3 alt rows. Now dec 1 st at neck edge on 3 foll alt rows.
Fasten off.
With WS of work facing, rejoin yarn to

sts left on spare needle and complete second side of neck to match first, reversing shapings.

BACK
Work as given for front to **.
Shape armholes
Keeping chart patt correct, cast off 1[2,3] sts at beg of next 2 rows, then dec 1 st at each end of next and every foll alt row until there are 43 sts.
Cast off.

SLEEVES
Using 2¼mm (US1) needles and yarn B, cast on 63[69,75] sts.
Work 14cm (5½in) K3, P1 rib as given for 2nd[1st,2nd] size of front.
Change to 3mm (US3) needles and commence patt from chart 1 as given for 2nd[1st,2nd] size of front.
When chart 1 is completed cont in st st in A only, inc 1 st at each end of next and every foll 5th row until there are 111[117,123] sts.
Work straight until sleeve measures 40[41,42]cm (16[16¼,16½]in) from top

of rib.
Commence patt from chart 2, work 2 rows.
Shape top
Keeping chart patt correct, cast off 1[2,3] sts at beg of next 2 rows, then dec 1 st at each end of next and every foll alt row until there are 17 sts.
Cast off.

MAKING UP
Join raglan seams.
Neckband
Using double-pointed 2¼mm (US1) needles and yarn B, with RS of work facing, K up 120 sts evenly around neck edge.
Work in rounds in K3, P1 rib as foll:
1st round (K3, P1) to end.
Rep this round until neckband measures 8cm (3in).
Cast off in rib.
Fold neckband in half on to WS and catch down.
Join side and sleeve seams.
Fold cuffs and lower rib in half on to WS and catch down.

CHART 1

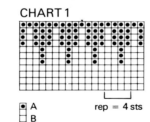

■ A
□ B

 rep = 4 sts

CHART 2

rep = 16 sts
3rd size front, 2nd size sleeves
1st size front
3rd size sleeve
2nd size front, 1st size sleeves

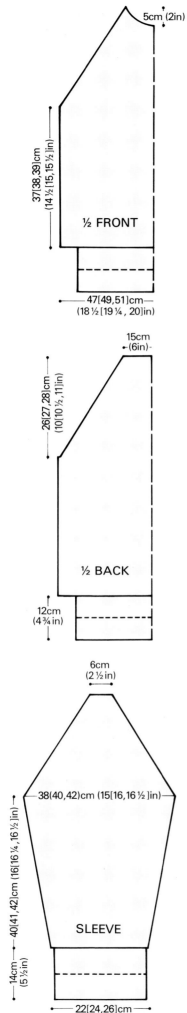

5cm (2in)

37[38,39]cm
(14½[15,15½]in)

½ FRONT

47[49,51]cm—
(18½[19¼ , 20]in)

15cm
←(6in)→

26[27,28]cm
(10[10½,11]in)

½ BACK

12cm
(4¾in)

6cm
(2½in)

38(40,42)cm (15[16,16½]in)

40[41,42]cm (16[16¼ , 16½]in)

SLEEVE

14cm
(5½in)

22[24,26]cm
(8½ [9½ ,10]in)

Alpine

A warm chunky sweater in a cable and garter-stitch pattern with bands of Fair Isle across the upper sleeves and yoke. The sleeves are worked from the shoulder down to the cuff.

WINTER
★ ★ ★

SIZES
To fit 96[101,106]cm (38[40,42]in) chest

MATERIALS
700[750,800]g (25[27,29]oz)
Aran-weight yarn in main colour (A)
200g (8oz) in contrast colour (B)
1 pair each 5mm (US8) and 6mm (US10) needles
Cable needle

TENSION
15 sts and 22 rows to 10cm (4in) over g st and cable panel on 6mm (US10) needles.

CABLE PANEL
Worked over 9 sts.
1st row (RS) Sl next 2 sts on to cable needle and hold at back of work, K2, then K2 from cable needle. P1, sl next 2 sts on to cable needle and hold at front of work, K2, then K2 from cable needle.
2nd and every alt row P to end.
3rd and 5th rows K4, P1, K4.
6th row P to end.
These 6 rows form the patt rep.

FRONT
Using 5mm (US8) needles and yarn A, cast on 83[87,91] sts.
Work 4cm (1½in) K1, P1 rib.
Change to 6mm (US10) needles and commence g st and cable panel patt as foll:
1st row (RS) K5, *work 1st row cable patt, K7[8,9]; rep from * to last 14 sts, work 1st row cable patt, K5.
2nd row K5, *work 2nd row cable patt, K7[8,9]; rep from * to last 14 sts, work 2nd row cable patt, K5.
These 2 rows set the position of cable panel and g st patt.
Cont in patt until work measures 32[33,34]cm (12½[13,13½]in) from top of rib, ending with a RS row.
Commence colour patt from chart 1, working in st st throughout, as foll:
1st–2nd rows Beg with a P row, work in st st in A.
3rd row Reading from right to left, patt to centre st, work centre st, then work chart patt in reverse.
4th row As 3rd row.
These 4 rows establish the chart patt.**
Cont in chart patt until work measures 48[50,52]cm (19[19½,20½]in), ending with a WS row.
Divide for neck
Next row Patt 34[36,38] sts, turn, leaving rem sts on a spare needle and cont on these sts only for first side of neck.
Keeping chart patt correct (when chart is completed cont in A only), cast off 2 sts at beg of next and 4 foll alt rows.
24[26,28] sts.
Work straight until front measures 53[55,57]cm (21[21¾,22½]in from top of rib.
Cast off.
With RS of work facing return to sts on spare needle, sl next 15 sts on to stitch holder, rejoin yarn to next st, patt to end.
Complete second side of neck to match first side, reversing shapings.

BACK
Work as given for front to **.
Cont in patt until chart is completed then cont in A only until work measures same as front to cast-off edge.
Cast off 24[26,28] sts at beg of next 2 rows.
Leave rem 35 sts on a stitch holder.

NECKBAND
Join right shoulder seam.
Using 5mm (US8) needles and yarn A, with RS of work facing, K up 17 sts down left side of front neck, K across 15 sts on st holder (inc 1 st at centre front), K up 17 sts up right side of front neck, K across 35 sts along back neck. 85 sts.
Work 2cm (¾in) K1, P1 rib.
Cast off in rib.

SLEEVES
Join left shoulder and neckband seam.
Using 6mm (US10) needles and yarn A, with RS of work facing, K up 65[69,73] sts between two points 21[22,23]cm (8¼[8½,9]in) on either side of shoulder seam.
Commence colour patt from chart 1, working in st st throughout, beg with a P row, and foll markers for sleeves, work 1st–11th rows, dec 1 st at each end of 8th row.
Now work in colour patt from chart 2 as foll:
1st row K4[6,8]B, patt 1st row chart 2 to centre st, work centre st, then work 1st row chart 2 in reverse, K4[6,8]B.

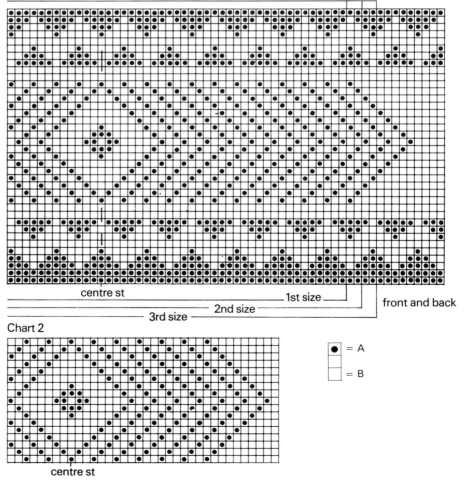

Chart 1

sleeve   1st 2nd 3rd size

centre st

3rd size
2nd size
1st size

front and back

Chart 2

centre st

● = A
□ = B

Designed by Soyzic Cornu Photograph: François Pompepui

Alpine

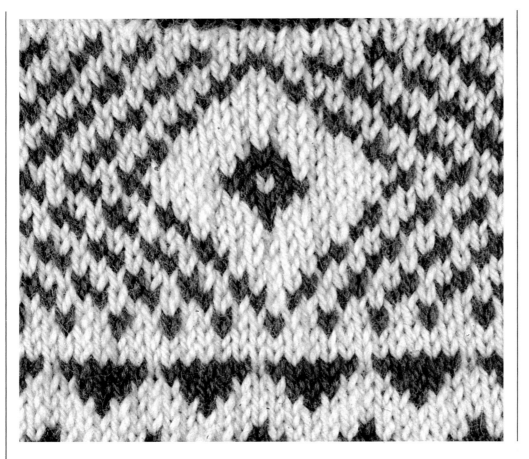

This row establishes the position of chart 2 with edge sts in B only.

Cont in patt, work 2nd–17th rows, then work 31st–38th rows of chart 1, *at the same time* dec 1 st at each end of 8th row from previous dec, and of 2 foll 8th rows. 57[61,65] sts.

When chart patt is completed, P 1 row in A, then cont in A and cable panel and g st patt as foll:

1st row K8[9,10], *work 1st row cable panel, K7[8,9]; rep from * to last 17[18,19] sts, work 1st row cable panel, K to end.

This row establishes position of cable panels.

Cont as set, *at the same time* dec 1 st at each end of 8th row from previous dec, and of every foll 8th row until 43[47,51] sts rem.

Work straight until sleeve measures 43[44,45]cm (17[17½,17¾]in) from K up row.

Change to 5mm (US8) needles and work 6cm (2½in) in K1, P1 rib.

Cast off in rib.

MAKING UP

Join side and sleeve seams.

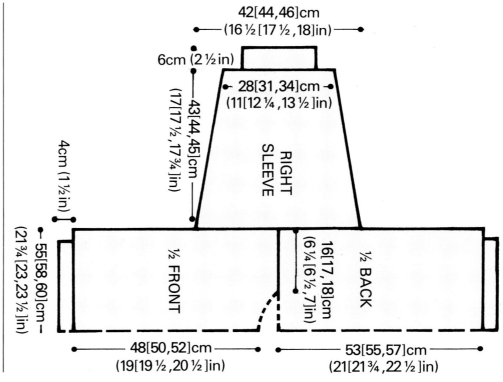

42[44,46]cm
(16½[17½,18]in)

6cm (2½in)

28[31,34]cm
(11[12¼,13½]in)

43[44,45]cm
(17[17½,17¾]in)

RIGHT SLEEVE

4cm (1½in)

55[58,60]cm
(21¾[23,23½]in)

½ FRONT

½ BACK

16[17,18]cm
(6¼[6½,7]in)

48[50,52]cm
(19[19½,20½]in)

53[55,57]cm
(21[21¾,22½]in)

Zigzag

A bold, sharp geometric design to help brighten up dark days. Knitted in a simple rib stitch in a fluffy mohair yarn in four colours.

SIZE
To fit up to 91cm (36in) bust

MATERIALS
200g (8oz) four-ply yarn in 1st colour (A)
150g (6oz) in 2nd colour (B)
100g (4oz) in 3rd colour (C)
50g (2oz) in 4th colour (D)
1 pair each 2¼mm (US1) and 3¼mm (US4) needles

TENSION
25 sts and 30 rows to 10cm (4in) over patt on 3¼mm (US4) needles.

FRONT
Using 2¼mm (US1) needles and C, cast on 154 sts.
Work in K2, P2 rib as foll:
1st row K2, *P2, K2; rep from * to end.
2nd row P2, *K2, P2; rep from * to end.
Rep last 2 rows until work measures 5cm (2in), ending with a 2nd row, *at the same time* dec 30 sts evenly across last row. 124 sts.
Change to 3¼mm (US4) needles and commence patt as foll:
1st row (RS) *K2, P1; rep from * to last st, K1.
2nd row K the P sts and P the K sts of previous row.
3rd row K1, *P1, K2; rep from * to end.
4th row As 2nd row.
These 4 rows form the patt rep.
Cont in patt until work measures 4cm (1½in) from top of rib, ending with a WS row.
Now cont in patt using colours as on chart as foll:
1st row (RS) Patt 120C, 4D.
2nd row Patt 4D, 120C.
3rd row Patt 116C, 8D.
4th row Patt 3A, 5D, 116C.
Cont in patt as set, reading RS rows from right to left and WS rows from left to right, until 109 rows have been worked from chart.
Divide for neck
Next row Patt 48 sts, cast off 28, patt to end.
Next row Patt to neck edge, turn, leaving rem sts on a spare needle and cont on these sts only for left side of neck. 48 sts.
Keeping chart and patt correct, cast off 5 sts at beg of next row and 4 sts at beg of foll alt row.
Now cast off 3 sts at beg of next alt row and then cast off 2 sts at beg of foll alt row.
Work 1 row.
Dec 1 st at beg of next row. 33 sts.
Work 2 rows straight, ending at armhole edge.

Shape shoulder
Cast off 11 sts at beg of next and foll alt row. Work 1 row.
Cast off rem 11 sts.
With RS facing rejoin yarn to sts on spare needle, work 2 rows straight then complete right side to match left reversing shapings and foll chart for patt.

BACK
Work as given for front, reversing patt as foll:
1st row (RS) Patt 4D, 120C.
2nd row Patt 120C, 4D.
Cont in this way, reading RS rows from left to right and WS rows from right to left, until 121 rows have been worked from chart.

111

Zigzag

Shape back neck
Next row Patt 49 sts, cast off 26 sts, patt to end.
Shape right shoulder and back neck
Next row Cast off 11 sts, patt to neck edge, turn, leaving rem sts on a spare needle and cont on these sts only for right side of neck. 38 sts.
Keeping chart correct, (cast off 8 sts at beg of next row and 11 sts at beg of foll row) twice.
With RS of work facing, rejoin yarn to sts on spare needle, patt to end.
Next row Cast off 11 sts, patt to end.
Complete to match first side of neck, reversing shaping.

RIGHT SLEEVE
Using 2¼mm (US1) needles and A, cast on 66 sts.
Work 5cm (2in) K2, P2 rib as given for front, dec 5 sts evenly across last row. 61 sts.
Change to 3¼mm (US4) needles and

work in patt as given for front, inc 1 st at each end of every foll 6th row until there are 99 sts.
Now work straight until sleeve measures 50cm (19½in) from top of rib.
Cast off in patt.

LEFT SLEEVE
Work as given for right sleeve using B instead of A.

MAKING UP
Join right shoulder seam.
Neckband
Using 2¼mm (US1) needles and B, with RS facing K up 142 sts evenly around neck edge.
Work 3cm (1¼in) K2, P2 rib as given for front.
Cast off in rib.
Join left shoulder and neckband seam.
Set sleeves in flat matching centre of cast-off edge of sleeve to shoulder seam.
Join side and sleeve seams.

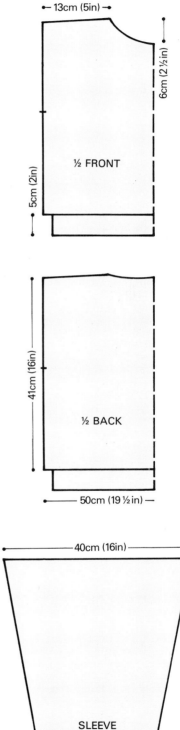

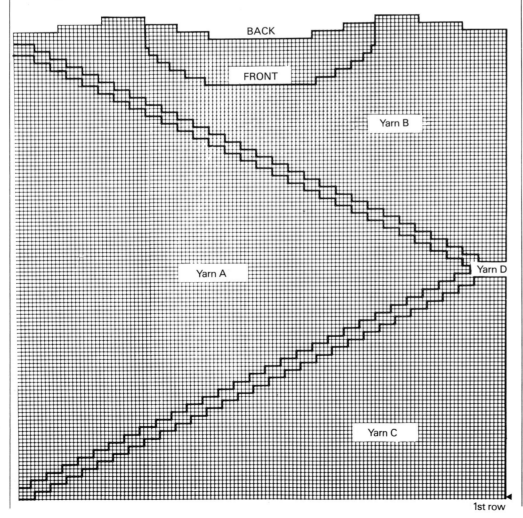

Designed by Valérie Ribadeau Dumas Photograph: Sepp

Equipment and Materials

One of the great advantages of knitting is that the equipment is simple, and the working materials are beautiful and varied.

THE NEEDLES

Knitting needles are the only really essential tools for all types of knitting. There are various kinds and most of them come in a range of sizes. In general, the thicker the yarn the larger the needle size used to work it. It is important to remember that the needle size quoted in a pattern is no more than a recommended size. It is intended to be used as a starting point for making tension samples. Many knitters will end up using a different size from the one specified.

TYPES OF NEEDLES

Single-pointed needles are the most common ones. They are sold in pairs and used for flat knitting. Nowadays they are usually made of a metal alloy but it is still possible to get plastic ones and many knitters find these more comfortable. As well as a full range of thicknesses they come in several lengths. Before beginning on a pattern, check whether it involves a large number of stitches. If it does, buy the longest needles.

Double-pointed needles come in sets of four or five and are used for knitting in the round. They come in a full range of thicknesses and several lengths. They can also be used for flat knitting so if a pattern lists a pair and a set of the same size needles, it may be possible to use two of the set instead of a pair.

Circular needles are sold singly. Each one consists of a pair of short pointed rods joined by a length of flexible wire. They come in a range of thicknesses and lengths and are used for knitting in the round, or for flat knitting where an exceptionally large number of stitches is involved.

Cable needles are used for working cable stitch patterns. They are short and double-pointed. Some are straight; others have a small kink or bend in the middle to help keep the stitches safely on the needle. They come in two thicknesses. Use the thinner ones with fine yarns and the thicker one with chunkier yarns. If a cable needle is needed for a particular pattern it will be listed along with the rest of the materials.

ACCESSORIES

Apart from the needles there are some other gadgets which will come in useful from time to time.

Stitch holders are rather like large safety pins and are used to hold stitches in waiting until they are needed at a later stage in the pattern. A spare needle or length of yarn will usually do the job just as well. For very small numbers of stitches an actual safety pin is ideal.

Row counters can be slotted on to the ends of single-pointed needles. They can help the knitter keep track of complicated stitch patterns.

Stitch stoppers are rubber or plastic guards that can be pushed onto the points of needles to prevent the stitches slipping off and unravelling.

Needle gauges are metal plates pierced with holes corresponding to international needle sizes. These are useful for measuring the size of needles, such as circular and double-pointed needles, that are not indelibly marked with their size.

Wool needles are sewing needles specially designed for sewing up knitted garments. They have rounded points that will not split the stitches.

Other items in general use that will be needed are a pair of sharp scissors, pins, a tape measure for taking body measurements and a rigid ruler for measuring the knitting itself.

NEEDLE SIZES

Metric	US	UK	Metric	US	UK
2mm	0	14	5mm	8	6
2¼mm	1	13	5½mm	9	5
2¾mm	2	12	6mm	10	4
3mm	3	11	6½mm	10½	3
3¼mm	4	10	7½mm	11	1
3¾mm	5	9	8mm	12	0
4mm	6	8	9mm	13	00
4½mm	7	7	10mm	15	000

THE YARNS

At one time 'yarn' was virtually synonymous with 'wool'. Now the range of yarns available to the knitter is bewilderingly wide and growing every year. Yarns made from some of the less common natural fibres – silk and linen, for example – are becoming more accessible in a wider selection of colours and finishes than ever before, and there are hundreds of new synthetic yarns of variable quality and properties, as well as novelty yarns and fancy threads which change with every season.

NATURAL FIBRES

Many knitters prefer to work only with natural fibres.

Wool, spun from sheep's fleece, is the most important of these. The best wool is 'pure new wool' which signifies that it has not previously been processed in any way. The best 'pure new wool' is often marked with the Woolmark, the symbol devised by the International Wool Secretariat to mark wool which reaches high standards in its class.

There are many different types of wool, its quality depending on the age and breed of the sheep as well as on the processing. Botany wool, which comes exclusively from merino sheep, is the softest, warmest type. Lambswool, also very fine and soft, comes from the 'first clip' of the young animal's fleece. Less soft, but very much stronger is the wool spun from semi-wild Cumbrian Herdwick sheep and from Jacob's sheep. These are usually only available in their natural colours – cream, through browns and greys to black. Shetland wool or 'fingering', spun from sheep raised in the Shetland Isles, is loosely twisted, light and warm. It is available in a range of colours and is especially suitable for traditional Shetland and Fair Isle patterns. In addition, there are highly specialised wools like the finest Shetland laceweight yarn handspun from wool plucked from the neck and back of the sheep, and 'bainin', the creamy coloured hardwearing yarn used for traditional Aran knitting. There is also a special tightly twisted wool made for knitting classic Guernseys. Wool of all types is the archetypal knitting yarn. It has all the desirable qualities – softness, warmth, strength and elasticity. It takes and holds dyes well and it's a sympathetic fibre to work with.

Mohair is another very popular yarn of animal origin. Spun from the hair of the Ankara goat, it is an unusually strong and hardwearing yarn which has the useful property of resisting dirt particles. However, the long fibres which account for its attractive, fluffy, slightly shiny appearance can irritate sensitive skin and it is rarely suitable for baby or children's clothes especially in its pure form. For this reason, and for reasons of cost, it is often found mixed with other softer and cheaper fibres.

Cashmere is another expensive goat hair yarn. The hairs are combed from Kashmiri goats in their moulting season and are especially light and soft. Though very comfortable to knit, it requires careful washing to avoid shrinkage.

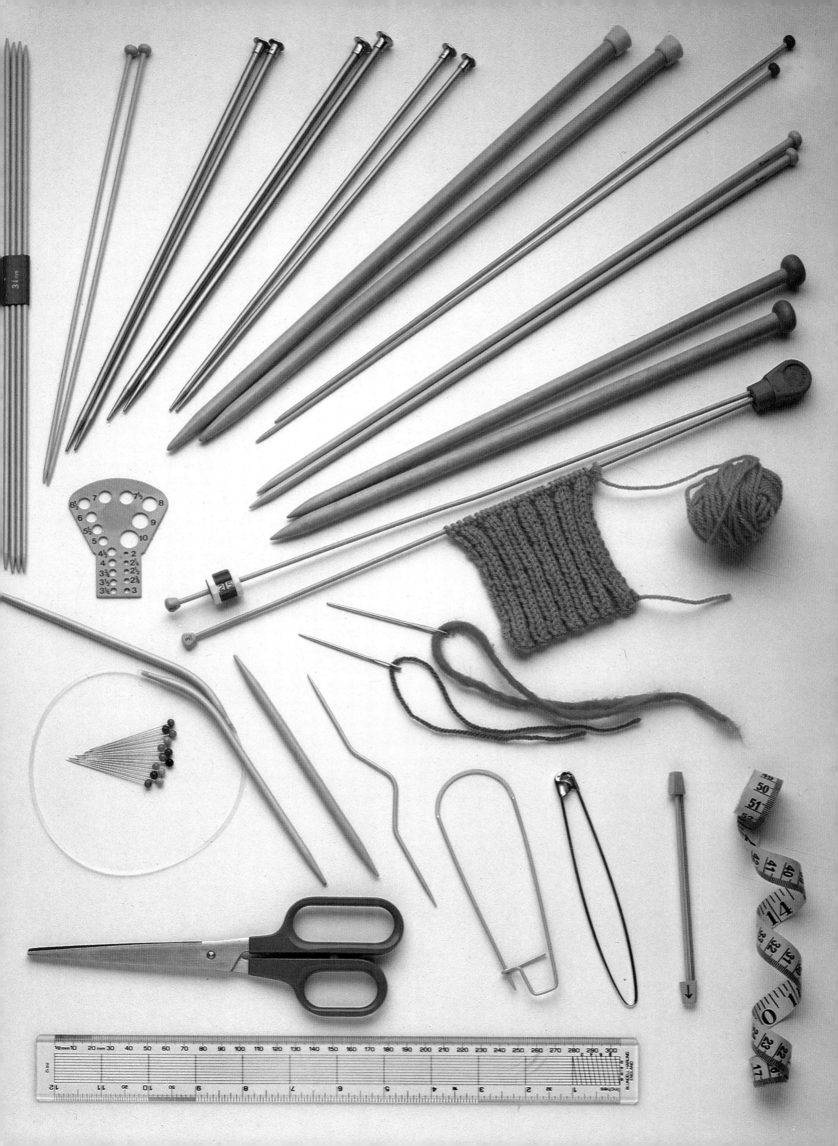

Alpaca is an increasingly common fibre of South American origin which is found in its pure form and mixed with other fibres especially wool. In its more usual natural state the colour ranges from creamy to dark brownish black, but it is also sometimes dyed.

Angora is produced from the fine silky coat of the Angora rabbit. It is a luxurious yarn with a definite glossy sheen which dyes well to soft pastels and deep rich shades. Making up can be a problem as the yarn is so slippery. The finish is fluffy, even shaggy, but unlike mohair it does not irritate the skin. The main disadvantage of angora is the cost.

Silk, also of animal origin, is produced by silk worms, the larvae of the silk moth. There are several kinds used for knitting, from the very shiny reeled silk to coarser slubbier tussah. It is the strongest of all the natural fibres and can be rather difficult to handle being at once slippery and harsh. Often it is mixed with other fibres. Wool and silk is a particularly compatible combination.

Cotton, made from the seed pod of a member of the mallow family, is the most important fibre of plant origin. It is very strong and durable and has the advantage of being cool in summer and fairly warm in winter. It is resistant to moths and is easily dyed. There is very little elasticity in the fibres so it is less comfortable to knit with than wool. It needs careful washing and a long drying period.

Linen is made from the flax plant and is second in strength only to silk. Like cotton it is moth-resistant and easily dyed. It is an expensive yarn and is often found in mixtures especially with cotton.

SYNTHETIC FIBRES

Many types of synthetic fibre are used in the manufacture of knitting yarns including nylon (polyamides), polyesters and acrylics. There are also fibres which, though not technically synthetic, since they originate in natural fibres (like wood pulp and cotton waste), are 'man-made'. The most important of these are viscose and triacetate. Being regenerated fibres they tend to be rather weak but they have other qualities which make them useful (the shininess of viscose, for example).

Most synthetic yarns are designed to duplicate the advantages of natural fibres and avoid the disadvantages. This they do with varying amounts of success. They are usually shrink-proof (in water) and moth- and mildew-resistant. However, they are often subject to heat damage and drying and pressing can be a problem. Though they do not felt in the same way as wool, for example, there is often a tendency to 'pilling' where small balls of fibres form on the surface of the fabric, and to static electricity which affects not only the feel of a garment but also the hang and the colour. Generally they are most successful when mixed with other, natural fibres.

TYPES OF YARN

Apart from the fibre composition one of the main factors affecting the nature of yarn is the way in which the fibres are processed or spun. Both natural and synthetic fibres are available in a range of finishes. There are the smooth plain classic yarns, which can be loosely twisted like Shetland yarn, medium-twisted like most conventional knitting wools, or tightly twisted like crêpe yarns and Guernsey 5-ply. The tighter the twist, the more tough and hardwearing the yarn will be. Cottons also vary: they can be soft and matt, or mercerised which makes them harder and shinier. Some yarn finishes are designed to produce different textures in the knitted fabric. Bouclé and loop yarns produce crunchy curly textures. Slub and flake yarns result in a knobbly uneven fabric. Chenille has a velvety finish. Then there are innumerable novelty yarns that combine fibres and colours in many different ways or which simulate other threads like gold and silver, ribbon or leather thonging.

SIZING

Most yarns are made up of several single strands twisted together. These single strands are known as plies and some of the yarns made from them are referred to by the number of plies they contain. This is a guide, though not an infallible guide, to the thickness of the yarn.

One-ply yarn is a scarce extremely fine yarn used for knitting exceptionally fine delicate Shetland 'ring' shawls and of limited use for other purposes.

Two-ply yarn is also very fine, but the traditional Shetland wool which knits 'as four-ply' is also technically two-ply.

Three-ply is a fine yarn used for making lightweight garments and baby clothes. Botany wool is often a three-ply yarn.

Four-ply is one of the most commonly used thicknesses. It is a fine lightweight yarn knitted on fairly small needles and particularly suitable for intricate colour-patterned garments like Fair Isle sweaters and for lacy stitches.

Double knitting is a very popular medium-weight yarn. It knits up more quickly than four-ply but is still fairly light and therefore suitable for a wide range of garments. It is often used for textures as well as colour patterns.

Aran-weight yarn is slightly thicker than double knitting and is used for outdoor garments as well as traditional Aran sweaters. Textured stitches show up particularly well in this weight.

Chunky yarn is another common type, thicker than Aran and used for heavy outdoor sweaters, jackets and coats. Some lighter but very loosely twisted bulky yarns (sometimes called *mèche* yarns) also 'knit as chunky'.

Many of the different fibres are available in all these thicknesses. Others are more limited. Cotton, for example, is rarely found thicker than double knitting and, for obvious reasons, the more expensive fibres like cashmere, alpaca and silk are not found in pure form in the heavier weights.

Key to yarns opposite
1 Random-dyed wool twisted with Lurex.
2 Space-dyed flake wool. 3 Undyed British Herdwick wool. 4 Undyed British Swaledale wool. 5 Fine glitter yarn. 6 Chunky Icelandic *mèche* wool. 7 Double knitting weight matt cotton. 8 Fine cashmere. 9 Double knitting weight mercerised cotton. 10 Five-ply Guernsey wool. 11 Fine soft cotton. 12 Wool and silk mixture. 13 Two-ply Shetland lace weight wool. 14 Pure silk. 15 Traditional Aran 'bainin' wool. 16 Dyed alpaca. 17 Chunky tweed wool. 18 Mohair. 19 Angora and lambswool mixture. 20 Two-ply Shetland jumper weight wool. 21 Cotton chenille.

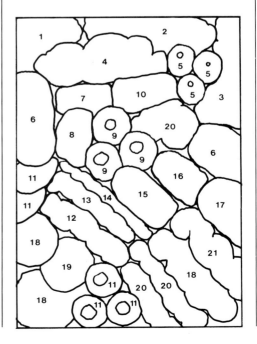

Choosing and Buying Yarn

Finding a suitable yarn is the first step towards making a successful garment.

In many cases the only choice available to the knitter is that of colour since the type and brand of yarn has been specified by the publisher of the pattern. While this is certainly the 'safest' course of action in that the result will be a garment almost identical to the one illustrated, it is also unnecessarily restricting, particularly in view of the wonderful yarns on sale nowadays.

In this book, only generic types of yarn have been listed in the materials section of each pattern. (For knitters who would like to obtain the original yarns, these are listed on page 128.) Yarns have been described by their approximate size or thickness – double knitting, Aran-weight, four-ply and so on – and, while this system has the advantage of flexibility and greater individuality in the finished garments, it does mean that the choice of yarn for each pattern must be exercised with much greater caution than usual. In particular, it means that the *quantities* given can only be *estimates*. It is also essential to choose a yarn that is suitable in terms of the type of garment and the stitch pattern and, most important of all, that will knit up to the required tension.

SUITABILITY

Out of the thousands of different yarns on the market only a dozen or so may be suitable for a particular garment. The fibre composition is important to the warmth, durability, cleaning requirements and to the 'handle' of a garment – whether it is soft or coarse to the touch. Many people are unable to wear certain rough fibres next to their skin which means that many types of wool and mohair are automatically excluded from the choice. It is unwise to use any of the hairier types of wool or mohair on children's or baby clothes.

The insulation properties of yarns vary considerably. For greatest warmth choose loosely twisted yarns with a high percentage of wool or mohair in them. Cashmere and angora are also noted for warmth. The coolest fibres are cotton and linen so choose these for summer garments. Synthetics, silk and tightly twisted yarns generally occupy the middle range. Many styles of garment are suitable for making in several different types of yarn, producing garments totally different in character from the same pattern. The sweater on page 28, for example, could be knitted in cotton for summer or spring, a loosely twisted Shetland yarn for winter or, for evening wear, in a metallic yarn.

TENSION CHART
Standard tension over stocking stitch using classic 100% wool yarns (number of stitches and rows to 10cm or 4in).

Needle size	4-ply sts	rows	Double knit sts	rows	Aran sts	rows	Chunky sts	rows
2¾mm (US2)	32	40	—	—	—	—	—	—
3mm (US3)	30	38	—	—	—	—	—	—
3¼mm (US4)	28	36	24	33	—	—	—	—
3¾mm (US5)	26	34	23	31	—	—	—	—
4mm (US6)	24	32	22	28	20	26	—	—
4½mm (US7)	—	—	21	26	19	24	—	—
5mm (US8)	—	—	20	25	18	22	—	—
5½mm (US9)	—	—	—	—	17	21	13	17
6mm (US10)	—	—	—	—	—	—	12	16

Another factor in the suitability of the yarn for its purpose is the finish or texture. Not all yarns are suitable for all stitch patterns. Some, like heavy bouclé, loop or slub yarns should only be used for plain simple stitches like stocking stitch and garter stitch. Lacy stitches and lightly textured stitches like basketweave and seed stitches would be totally obscured by such yarns. Most textured stitch patterns should be worked in plain smooth yarns. If the stitch is heavily embossed then lightly fluffy or flecked yarns can be effective. Delicate, fluffy yarns are particularly suitable for lacy patterns. Lace stitches usually also work well in cotton. Cables and crossover patterns show up best in fairly plain yarns, either smooth or brushed. Bold multi-coloured patterns (page 111, for example) can be worked in yarns with some surface texture such as light bouclé, mohair and slub yarns. More intricate patterns with small motifs are best in smooth yarns that display the fine detail of the pattern.

TENSION
Correct tension is the most important single factor in the success of any knitted garment. If the knitter does not match the tension specified in the pattern the garment will simply be too big or too small. (See page 122 for detailed information on measuring, checking and adjusting tension.) When choosing yarn it is essential to find one that can be knitted up to the tension given in the pattern. In virtually every case this will entail choosing a yarn in the same size group as that specified, but it does not mean that each and every double knitting yarn or four-ply yarn can be knitted up to the tension given for a particular double knitting or four-ply in a particular pattern. Yarns can vary a great deal as to tension even if they belong to the same group. The tension table given opposite is an average only. The actual figures can be as much as two or three stitches or rows more or less. The only sure way of finding out whether it is possible to achieve a particular tension with a particular yarn is to knit up a sample and measure it. Before you get to that stage however, there is often a good deal of information on labels and ball bands that helps narrow the choice.

READING BALL BANDS
Most modern yarn labels are very informative. At their best they display the fibre content, washing and pressing symbols, shade number, dye lot number, weight of the ball in metric and standard measures, length of thread also in metric and standard measures and of course, the name of the manufacturer and the brand name of the yarn. The description of the yarn may include its thickness (double knitting, for example) or it may simply be a fanciful but relatively meaningless name. In any case, there may also be a recommended needle size and tension measurement. This is the tension which, in the manufacturer's view, produces the correct handle in the knitted fabric – neither so tight that the yarn is stretched and damaged and the fabric stiff, nor so loose that it has little

body or shape. If this measurement is near that given in the pattern then it is likely that the given tension can be achieved either on the same or a different needle size. When making the comparison check that both tensions are quoted over the same stitch pattern. On ball bands it is almost always stocking stitch.

The ball band is less helpful if, as often happens, the pattern designer has deliberately chosen to use a yarn at an unorthodox tension in order to achieve a specific effect. In this case there is no alternative to buying a ball of yarn and making up a sample. If, by sampling or checking the ball band, it is impossible to achieve the correct row and stitch tension, choose a yarn that will give you the correct stitch tension and adjust the length by working more or fewer rows.

QUANTITY
Having found a yarn which has a suitable fibre composition and finish, and which will knit up to the correct tension the only remaining problem is that of quantity: how much of this yarn will it take to complete the garment. Each pattern lists an amount of yarn, but this is only an approximation based on the amount of the original yarn that was required. You may need more or less of the new yarn, especially if the fibre content or finish is different.

The amount of yarn needed to complete a garment is directly related to the length of the thread. However, yarn is sold by weight and the length of yarn per 25g (1oz) ball varies according to the thickness of the yarn, its fibre content and finish. The 'heaviest' yarns are cotton and linen, followed by wool, mohair and, finally, the lightest yarns, the synthetics. There is more length for the same weight in wholly synthetic yarns and, for this reason, they are said to 'go further'. The length of the thread is also affected by the finish. A tightly twisted yarn has less length per 25g (1oz) than a loosely twisted yarn made of the same fibres and novelty yarns with a lot of extra curls, knobbles and slubs are

relatively heavier than smooth yarns so you will need relatively more of these.

ESTIMATING QUANTITY
The only sure way of knowing the exact amount needed for a specific garment is to knit it up, by which time it is too late to find that you haven't enough. A reasonable estimate can be made by knitting up a single ball in the correct stitch pattern and tension and using that as a basis for calculating the remaining amount. Divide the total area of the garment (worked out from the measurement diagram) by the area that can be knitted with one ball to give you the total number of balls needed.

In practice, when buying yarn it is often possible to obtain advice from the shop itself on the amount needed for a particular garment. Specialist shops are also usually quite willing to reserve yarn against the possibility that it will be needed later. If you have to buy it all at once, the table given below should give you some guidance. Use it together with the information on the ball band and with the estimate given in the pattern. If in doubt always buy more than you think you will need. Any left over can be used for repair jobs or for knitting stitch samples.

DYE LOT
Make sure that all the yarn you buy comes from the same dye lot as there is a remarkable amount of difference between them even in 'no-colour' colours like black and white. While this may not be seen when the yarn is in the ball it becomes glaringly obviously when it is knitted up.

Approximate yarn requirement for a long-sleeved round-necked sweater, size 91cm (36in) bust or chest, knitted in stocking stitch.

Yarn thickness	Fibre content	Number of 25g (1oz) balls
3-ply	100% cotton	20
	100% wool	14
	75% acrylic/25% wool	14
4-ply	100% cotton	22
	100% wool	16
	75% acrylic/25% wool	14
	100% acrylic	12
Double knitting	100% cotton	26
	50% wool/50% silk	20
	100% wool	18
	75% acrylic/25% wool	16
	70% mohair/30% acrylic	16
Aran	100% wool	24
	75% acrylic/25% wool	20
	60% acrylic/40% mohair	16
Chunky	100% wool	32
	75% acrylic/25% wool	28
	60% acrylic/40% mohair	24

Reading the Patterns

To the uninitiated the language of knitting patterns is meaningless but after a while it's easy to find your way about.

All knitting patterns contain the same kinds of information but the way that information is conveyed can vary. Differences of punctuation, abbreviation and the way charts, for example, are laid out can be confusing. This section is specifically intended to help you read the patterns in this book, but some of it will also be helpful with other patterns.

All knitting patterns should contain the following types of information: the size of the finished garment, a list of the materials and equipment required to make it, a tension measurement, a key to the abbreviations used, a set of working instructions for each part of the garment, which may include charts as well as written instructions, and finally a guide to making up and finishing the garment. In most cases there will also be a sketch or photograph of the garment. In this book there is also a star rating which will give the knitter some idea of the level of difficulty involved in the pattern. This is explained on page 7.

SIZE
Most of the patterns in this book provide instructions for several sizes. The instructions for different sizes are separated by square brackets. The first section of each pattern indicates what sizes are provided for and how those sizes are to be displayed. For example, where, as in most instances, there are three sizes the first size is given first before the brackets, followed by the second size and then the third size inside a set of square brackets thus: 1st size[2nd size, 3rd size]. This means that where in the pattern there is a set of instructions given in similar formation, the instructions given before the brackets must be followed for the first size, and those inside the brackets for the second and third sizes. Where there are no brackets, the instructions are the same for all sizes.

The sizes quoted in this section are always 'to fit' sizes, given in terms of a bust or chest measurement for adults and an age for children. These sizes are given in metric measurements, with standard measurement equivalents following in parentheses. The 'to fit' measurement includes an allowance for ease of movement or tolerance in the garment, which can range from a small amount for a close-fitting garment to quite a lot for something loose and baggy. The actual measurements of the finished garment are given on a measurement diagram like the one on the right or, in the case of garments

knitted in the round, under the 'to fit' measurement. When deciding which size to knit, look at the actual measurements as well as the to fit measurement. You may well decide to knit a larger or smaller size. The measurement diagram will also help you discover whether you need to make any adjustments to the pattern before you begin or during the course of the work.

MATERIALS
The list of materials includes the yarn, size and type of needles, including cable needles, and anything else in the way of buttons, zips or trimmings needed to complete that particular garment. It does not include all the ancillary items that are always needed like tape measure, scissors, stitch holders and sewing up needles. In this book the patterns specify general types of yarn rather than specific brands so the quantities given can only be approximate. Read the information on pages 118–19 before buying the yarn. Remember also that the needle sizes given in these patterns are also estimated, and the size you should use depends on your tension check.

Where more than one colour or type of yarn is used these are coded A, B, C and so on in the list of materials. These codes will be used throughout the instructions.

TENSION
It is vital to check your tension before embarking on the pattern. This is explained in detail on page 122.

ABBREVIATIONS
All knitting patterns are written in abbreviated form in order to save space

and avoid much tedious repetition. The abbreviations used in this book are listed on page 7. With some patterns there is also a list of special abbreviations that are relevant only to that pattern. Where, in the course of the pattern, there is an instruction to 'inc' or 'dec' a certain number of stitches without any further detail, any appropriate method of increasing or decreasing may be used.

WORKING INSTRUCTIONS
Unless the garment is made in one piece the working instructions are usually divided up under appropriate headings for the separate pieces – back, front, sleeves and so on. These correspond to the sections shown in the measurement diagram. Work them in the order in which they are printed since the instructions for any stitch pattern used are often fully laid out only in the first section. Thereafter it will simply be referred to as 'patt'. Where several different stitch patterns are arranged in vertical panels on a garment, these patterns may be laid out quite separately before the actual working instructions for each section begin. They are referred to as panel patterns and are a means of simplifying what would otherwise be very lengthy instructions. It can be helpful to familiarise yourself with panel patterns by making samples before beginning work on the garment itself. Otherwise they can be ignored until you are instructed to refer to them during the course of the work.

Read right through the working instructions before you begin. Make sure that you understand the meaning of all the abbreviations used in the pattern

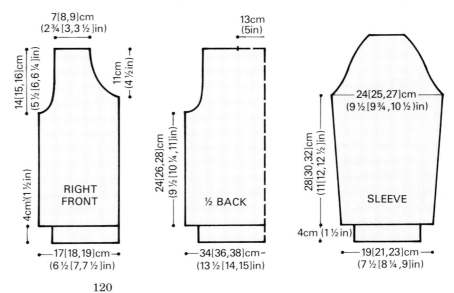

and that you are familiar with the basic stitches whose instructions are not given in detail. It is assumed that most knitters know how to work stocking stitch, garter stitch, reverse stocking stitch, moss stitch and K1, P1 and K2, P2 rib. Those who do not should read the instructions on page 123.

All knitting patterns involve repeats. It may be necessary to repeat a sequence of stitches during a row, or a sequence of rows, or shaping instructions, or whole sections of a pattern. These repeats are signalled in a variety of ways. In this book, repeats are marked by asterisks or parentheses. The use of asterisks is self-explanatory ('rep from * to end of row' or 'rep from ** to **' for example). In the case of parentheses, the instruction inside the parentheses should be repeated the number of times stated immediately after them (for example, '(K2 tog) 8 times'). Where there is a complete sequence of instructions inside the parentheses the whole sequence should be repeated the stated number of times (as in '(K1, P3, K4) 8 times').

CHARTS

Two types of chart can appear as part of the working instructions – stitch pattern charts and colourwork charts. In theory the whole of a knitting pattern can be charted through, in this book, none of the patterns fall into that category. Both stitch and colourwork charts are in the form of a grid where one stitch is represented by one square, and a row of stitches by a row of squares. All the charts are worked from the bottom upwards. The first row to be worked is usually the bottom row of the chart and is always marked as '1st row'. A chart may represent a motif to be worked only

once on a section of the garment, or it may represent a pattern to be repeated either horizontally or vertically or both. In any case, the written instructions will inform you where to place the charted motif or pattern. In some cases the first few rows of the chart will also be written out in full, in others you may be instructed to work from one point on the chart to another.

The same chart can be used for flat and circular knitting though it will be read differently. For flat knitting, read right-side rows from right to left and wrong-side rows from left to right. In circular knitting, every row on the chart represents a round of knitting and all rows must be read from right to left. Unless otherwise indicated, all colourwork charts should be worked in stocking stitch.

All charts are accompanied by a key that explains the meaning of the symbols used in the chart. Each symbol refers either to the type of stitch that should be worked or to the colour that should be used for the stitch. In some cases it refers to both. The colour codes used in the key are those used in the list of materials.

MAKING UP

This section describes how to put together the various pattern pieces and is described in full on pages 124–25.

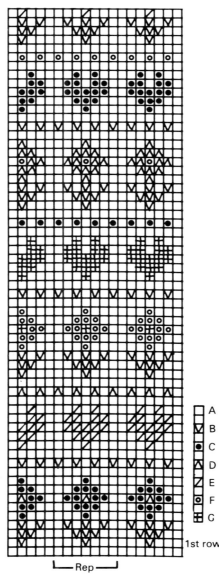

Rep

1st row

	A
	B
	C
	D
	E
	F
	G

NOTES FOR AMERICAN KNITTERS
American knitters will have few problems in working from English patterns and *vice versa*. The main difficulties arise from some differences in terminology and the fact that knitting in the UK has become entirely metricated. The patterns provide instructions in both metric and standard measurements. The following charts should also prove useful.

TERMINOLOGY

UK	US
cast off	bind off
catch down	tack down
double crochet	single crochet
stocking stitch	stockinette stitch
Swiss darning	duplicate stitch
tension	gauge
yarn forward	yarn over or yarn to front
yarn over needle	yarn over
yarn round needle	yarn over

All other terms are the same in both countries.

US/UK YARN EQUIVALENTS

UK	US
Four-ply	Sport
Double knitting	Knitting worsted
Aran-weight	Fisherman
Chunky	Bulky

These yarns are approximate equivalents only. It is still essential to check your tension.

METRIC CONVERSION TABLES

Length (to the nearest ¼in)		Weight (rounded up to the nearest ¼oz)	
cm	in	g	oz
1	½	25	1
2	¾	50	2
3	1¼	100	3¾
4	1½	150	5½
5	2	200	7¼
6	2½	250	9
7	2¾	300	10¾
8	3	350	12½
9	3½	400	14¼
10	4	450	16
11	4¼	500	17¾
12	4¾	550	19½
13	5	600	21¼
14	5½	650	23
15	6	700	24¾
16	6¼	750	26½
17	6¾	800	28¼
18	7	850	30
19	7½	900	31¾
20	8	950	33¾
25	9¾	1000	35½
30	11¾	1200	42¼
35	13¾	1400	49¼
40	15¾	1600	56¼
45	17¾	1800	63½
50	19¾	2000	70½

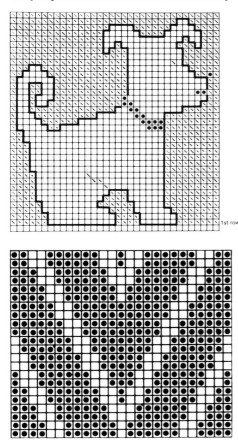

1st row

● P   □ K

Tension

Correct tension is vitally important, yet it is something often disregarded even by experienced knitters.

All knitting patterns are accompanied by a tension measurement. This refers to the number of stitches and rows there are to a given measurement – usually 10cm (4in) – and is the basis on which all the pattern calculations have been made. Unless this tension is matched by the knitter the garment will not be the correct size.

Tension is affected by several factors. Two of them – needle size and stitch pattern – are also specified in the tension measurement given in every pattern. The third, yarn, is assumed to be the yarn specified in the materials section of the pattern and will not be mentioned in the tension measurement unless there are several yarns or other special circumstances (such as the yarn being used double). The fourth factor, and the one most ignored, is the knitter.

STITCH PATTERN
Different stitch patterns produce different tensions, even where the needle size, yarn and knitter remain the same. This is obvious when comparing stitches like lace and rib that are totally different in character. Lace patterns are very open and loose and have fewer stitches to 10cm (4in) than ribs, which are designed to pull inwards and have more stitches to 10cm (4in). However, it is also true of stitch patterns that are ostensibly similar like, for example, garter stitch and stocking stitch. As a result you cannot substitute a new stitch for the one given in a pattern and assume that the overall measurements will stay the same. When checking your tension for a particular pattern the stitch pattern specified in the tension measurement must be used for the tension sample.

NEEDLE SIZE
Since tension is, in effect, a measure of the size of individual stitches the size of the needles is obviously directly linked. The larger the needles the larger will be the stitches and the looser the tension – there will be fewer stitches and rows to the centimetre (inch). Smaller needles produce tighter tension and therefore more stitches and rows to the measurement.

YARN
Patterns worked in thicker yarns will have fewer stitches and rows to the measurement than those worked in finer yarns. A careful tension check is even more vital when patterns specify only generic types of yarn, as in this book.

THE KNITTER
The effect of the individual knitter on tension is often underestimated, yet it is as important as any of the other factors. It is the knitter who controls the flow of yarn through the fingers, putting more or less tension on the thread. Some people naturally knit more loosely than others. Tension is an entirely personal thing like a signature. For this reason it is not advisable for two people to work on different parts of the same garment. If they do, each knitter should check her or his tension independently of the other one. They may well need to use different needle sizes to achieve correct tension.

The tension measurement given in the pattern is the tension of the designer of the pattern and is quite likely to be different from that of the individual knitter. However, in order to complete the pattern successfully and produce a garment with the correct measurements, it is essential for the knitter to adjust her or his tension to match that of the pattern. This cannot be done by attempting to knit more tightly or more loosely than usual. It must be done by changing to a smaller or larger needle size. The needle size stated in the materials and tension section of patterns is never more than a rough guide to the size that should actually be used. It is a recommended starting point for making tension samples. In many cases it will be necessary to use a different size. In such cases, if larger or smaller needles are used for other parts of the pattern (the rib, for example) these must also be adjusted in the same direction.

MAKING A TENSION SAMPLE
In order to check your tension it is necessary to make tension samples. Using the recommended needle size and the yarn specified in the materials

section of the pattern (or in the tension measurement if there is more than one type of yarn), knit up a square in the stitch pattern given in the tension measurement. Cast on a few more stitches than the figure given for the stitch tension and work a few more rows than the figure given for the row tension. Cast off as usual and block and press the sample as instructed in the making up section of the pattern or on the ball band of the yarn.

MEASURING TENSION
Place the sample on a flat surface. Take a rigid ruler and place it horizontally on the sample, lining it up along the bottom of a row of stitches. Mark the zero point with a pin on the left-hand side of a stitch. Mark the 10cm (4in) point with another pin. Count the number of stitches between the pins including half stitches if any. This will give you the figure for the stitch tension.

Now place the ruler vertically on the sample aligning it along one side of a column of stitches. Pin the zero and 10cm (4in) points. Count the number of rows between the pins to give the figure for the row tension of the sample. If there are fewer stitches and rows than those given for the pattern tension, the sample is too loose. Knit up a sample using the next smallest needle size and measure it again. If there are too many rows and stitches, the sample is too tight. Knit up a sample using the next largest size and measure it again. Carry on in this way, changing the size of the needles until the tension of the pattern is matched. Occasionally it is impossible to match both stitch and row tension. In such cases choose a needle size that will give you the correct stitch tension, working more or fewer rows to adjust the length.

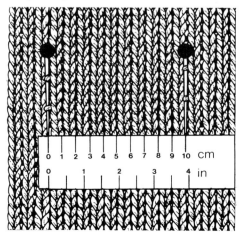

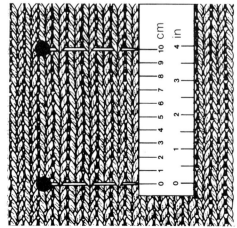

BASIC STITCHES

Most of the tension measurements in this book are given over basic stitches involving straightforward combinations of knit and purl stitches. It is assumed in the patterns that knitters know these stitches by heart. For those who do not, here is a brief refresher course on how to work them. Unless otherwise stated, the stitch patterns can be worked over any number of stitches.

Garter stitch is worked by knitting every stitch of every row, producing a fabric with marked horizontal ridges. It can also be worked by purling every stitch of every row. In circular knitting the rounds are knitted and purled alternately. To obtain a neat edge in garter stitch when it is used for borders, slip the edge stitch on every alternate row.

Stocking stitch is worked by knitting every stitch in right-side rows and purling every stitch in wrong-side rows. It produces a smooth fabric that curls inwards and is suitable for the body of a garment but not usually for the edges. In circular knitting every round is knitted.

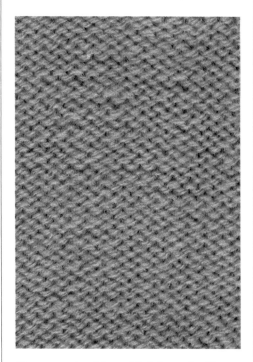

Reverse stocking stitch is worked by purling every stitch in right-side rows and knitting every stitch in wrong-side rows. In circular knitting all the rows are purled.

K1, P1 rib Sometimes called single rib, this stitch is worked by knitting and purling stitches alternately in the first row. In every subsequent row the stitches that were knitted the previous row are purled and the stitches that were purled are knitted. In circular knitting the same stitches are purled or knitted in every round. In flat knitting K1, P1 rib can be worked over an odd or even number of stitches. In circular knitting it can only be worked over an even number of stitches.

K2, P2 rib Sometimes called double rib, this stitch is worked by knitting and purling pairs of stitches alternately in the first row. In every subsequent row knit the stitches that were purled the previous row and purl the stitches that were knitted. In circular knitting the same stitches are knitted or purled in every round. In flat knitting K2, P2 rib must be worked over an even number of stitches. In circular knitting it must be worked over a multiple of four stitches.

Moss stitch is suitable for the body of a garment and for borders. It is worked by knitting and purling stitches alternately in the first row. In all subsequent rows the stitches that were knitted the previous row are again knitted and the stitches that were purled are again purled. In circular knitting the stitches that were knitted the previous row are purled and the stitches that were purled are knitted. In flat knitting moss stitch can be worked over any number of stitches. In circular knitting it must be worked over an even number of stitches.

Making Up

Extra care in making up will give a garment a professional finish.

That depressing 'homemade' look so common in handknits is often the result of careless making up. Many knitters devote endless time and patience to their knitting but rush the making up process in their eagerness to be finished. Time spent at this stage means that all the labours of the previous days, weeks or even months will not be wasted. The making up section of a pattern tells you how to seam the various pieces together and in what order. But before you even begin to join seams there are several important processes to go through that most patterns do not bother to mention.

ENDS

During the course of the knitting it will have been necessary to join in a new ball of yarn several times. Unless the yarn ends have been spliced together there will be many long loose ends which have to be darned in. These should be at the edges of each piece since it is usual to join in a new ball of yarn at the beginning of a row rather than in the middle. Darn in each end separately up the sides of the knitting or along edges that will be seamed. Try to avoid darning ends into the centre as this can show on the right side. Do not simply knot the ends and cut them off as they can work loose during wear. Darn in at least 5cm (2in) of every end.

BLOCKING

All the component pieces of the garment must be pinned out to the correct shape and measurements before seaming. This process is called blocking. Fold a white towel or blanket to make a smooth pad and place it on a flat hard surface. Place the garment pieces wrong side up on the pad and pin it out all round, checking the measurements of each part against the measurement diagram as you do so. Slight discrepancies in the measurements can often be adjusted by stretching or easing the knitting just a little. Make sure that edges that should

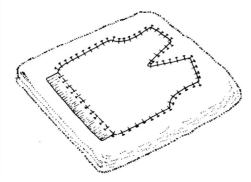

be straight are pinned out straight and that curves and other shaped edges are smooth. Push the pins into the pad right up to the head, spacing them a short distance apart. Do not pin around ribbed edges. These should be allowed to pull in naturally. Pin along the join between the ribbed sections and the rest.

PRESSING

Check the pressing instructions on the ball band of the yarn. The symbols below are the relevant ones. Many yarns, especially synthetics, should not be pressed at all as they will suffer heat damage or the finish will be adversely affected. Garments worked in such yarns can be sprayed lightly with water and allowed to dry into shape. If the yarn can be pressed, cover the blocked garment with a clean white cloth – damp for wool, dry for synthetics and mixtures. Using the appropriate heat setting, press the knitting using up and down rather than sliding movements. Very few garments benefit from heavy pressing so use a light touch and do not hold the iron on the garment for any length of time. Do not press garter stitch or ribbing or textured patterns. Leave to dry naturally before removing the pins.

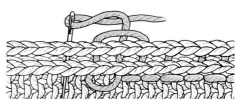

Do not iron Cool (120°C)

Warm (160°C) Hot (210°C)

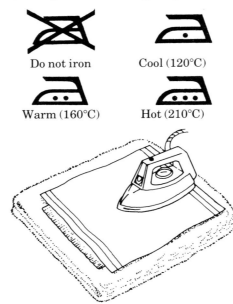

SEAMS

Work the seams in the order given in the making up section of the pattern. There is usually a good reason for it. There may, for example, be a neckband to work. This will necessitate first joining one of the shoulder seams so that it can be worked in one piece and it is easier to do this before the side seams have been

joined. Some knitters prefer to work neckbands in the round. In this case, both shoulders should be joined first.

If possible join seams with the same yarn as that used for the knitting. If the yarn is very thick or textured use a finer smooth yarn in the same colour. When working any seam take care not to split the knitted stitches. Use a round-ended wool needle and insert it between or through the centre of stitches rather than through the yarn itself.

The choice of seam is generally left up to the knitter. There are several that are suitable for joining knitted garments. **Backstitch** seams are very strong but can be bulky. Use them for shoulder seams and for setting in sleeves. Work the seam one stitch from the edge.

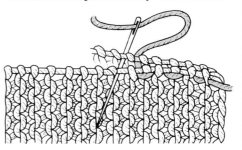

Flat seams are used to join on borders such as buttonbands and buttonhole bands that have been made separately and where the join is likely to be visible.

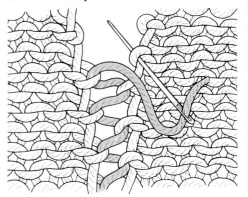

Invisible seams are ideal for joining the side seams of garments made in stocking stitch. They are worked with the right side facing and from the bottom of the seam to the top.

GRAFTING

Grafting produces a completely invisible join but it can only be used on straight horizontal edges with an equal number of stitches in each edge. If a join is to be grafted do not cast off the stitches on each edge. Place one set of stitches on a spare needle with the point on the right and the other on a spare needle with the point on the left. Now position the needles so that both are pointing to the right and the stitches are opposite each other. Thread a wool needle with matching yarn and graft the two sets of stitches together as shown. The grafting thread in the diagram is in a contrast colour to make it clearer. As each stitch is secured with the grafting thread withdraw the needle from it. Take care to match the original tension.

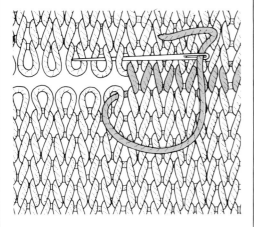

SWISS DARNING

The making up stage is the time when any additional embroidery, beading or other decoration is worked on the garment. Any of the more conventional embroidery stitches can be used on knitwear but there is also a stitch which is special to it. Swiss darning imitates the form of stocking stitch. Worked in matching yarn it is a useful reinforcing technique. Worked in contrast colours it enables you to work colour patterns and motifs on knitwear that look as if they have been knitted in. The Swiss darning stitches must cover the knitted background stitches completely if they are to be fully effective so use a yarn that is the same weight as the original one.

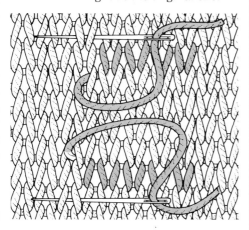

SETTING IN SLEEVES

There are four main sleeve types common in knitted garments: raglan, set-in, flat and French. They are all made up in different ways though the pattern may only say, 'Set in sleeves.'

Raglan seams are joined before the side seams. Sometimes three of the seams are joined first leaving one of the back ones open, then a neckband is knitted and the fourth seam joined. The underarm and side seams are joined in one.
Set-in sleeves are usually made up separately and then joined to the body of the garment. Join the shoulder and side seams, then join the underarm seam. With the sleeve turned right side out and the body wrong side out fit the sleeve in position matching the underarm seam with the side seam and the sleeve head with the shoulder seam. Pin round the armhole easing in any fullness round the sleeve head. Join the armhole seam with a backstitch seam.
Flat sleeves have no shaping on the sleeve head, nor is there shaping on the body. Join the shoulder seams. Place the centre of the cast-off edge of the sleeve to the shoulder seam. Join the armhole seam, then the side and underarm seams.
French sleeves have no shaping on the sleeve head and there is only simple cast-off shaping on the body. Join the shoulder seam. Place the centre of the cast-off edge of the sleeve to the shoulder seam and join the straight part of the armhole seam. Now join the cast-off stitches at the underarm to the last few rows of the sleeve.

POCKETS

The nature of the making up process for pockets depends on whether it is a patch pocket, or a pocket that is set in horizontally, vertically or into the side seams. If a pattern does not include instructions for a pocket it is very easy to make a patch or side seam pocket.
Patch pockets can be made either in the same yarn and stitch pattern as the main part of the garment or in a contrast. Often they are square or rectangular but they can be any shape. The edging of the pocket opening is made at the same time as the rest of the pocket. It should be in a suitable border stitch like rib, moss stitch or garter stitch. Sew the pocket on during the making up stage either decoratively with bold embroidery stitches or invisibly, using either neat slipstitching or, for a very firm and totally invisible join, in Swiss darning through both thicknesses in a matching yarn. This latter join only works if the pocket and background are in stocking stitch.
Horizontal pockets are knitted into the garment during the course of the work. The pocket lining may also be knitted in or it can be worked separately and sewn in afterwards. During the making up stage it is usually necessary to attach the pocket lining to the inside of the garment using neat slipstitching in a matching yarn, and to work a pocket edging. Slipstitch the row ends of the pocket edging to the right side.
Vertical pockets are also knitted in as you go along and the lining either made separately or knitted in. When slipstitching the lining to the inside of the garment make sure it is aligned with the first and last rows of the pocket opening to avoid puckering.
Side seam pockets are common on jackets and cardigans. The lining is made separately in the form of a rectangular bag and the opening of the bag is stitched into the seam, half to the back of the garment and half to the front. Often there is no edging, and the opening is buttoned or zipped.

BUTTONS

Choose buttons that are slightly bigger than the actual measurement of the buttonhole and make sure they are not too heavy for the fabric. Sew them on with the yarn used for the garment or, if it is too bulky, in a finer matching yarn. The edges of the buttonhole can, if required, be reinforced by working buttonhole stitch round the edges.

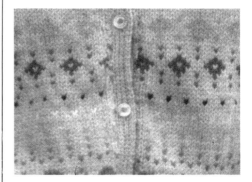

ZIPS

Zips are often used to close front openings of jackets or cardigans and for pocket tops. The required length is usually specified in the materials. If the length of the garment has been altered, remember to buy a different length zip. It should be slightly shorter rather than longer than the actual length of the opening. Insert the zip closed, making sure that both sides of the opening match and that the edges of the knitting do not overlap the zip teeth. Pin it in position, stretching it slightly if necessary (never stretch the knitting to fit the zip). Fold in the extra tape at the top and backstitch in place.

Aftercare

The life of knitted garments can be prolonged by giving special attention to washing and cleaning.

Hand knitting is a pleasurable but time-consuming craft and the materials involved are relatively expensive so it makes a good deal of sense to look after your garments really well. Whatever the yarn used all knitwear requires very careful washing and cleaning. Even those yarns marked 'easy-care' and 'machine washable' benefit from more gentle handling from time to time. In order to choose the correct cleaning method it is essential to know the fibre composition of the yarn. The ball band should contain this information and it may also display the symbols of the International Textile Care Labelling Code, as reproduced here.

DRY-CLEANING
Many yarns, including wool, can be dry-cleaned and this can be a very practical solution where time is short. However, repeated dry-cleaning eventually removes the softness of the yarn and the elasticity of ribbing so it is advisable to wash such garments occasionally to restore these properties. Some synthetic yarns and mixtures need special care during dry-cleaning. Check the label and make sure the dry-cleaner has the relevant information.

WASHING
Unless the ball band contains specific information to the contrary all knitwear

should be hand-washed. It is also safest to hand-wash any garment where the fibre content of the yarn is unknown. Careless washing, either by machine or by hand, causes the fibres of the yarn to mat together or 'felt'. This is particularly true of yarns made from pure animal fibres like wool, alpaca and mohair. There is no remedy for felting but it can be considerably delayed and often prevented indefinitely by careful, gentle hand-washing.

Friction is one of the many causes of felting so wash knitwear frequently to avoid the necessity of rubbing to remove ingrained dirt. Use a detergent specially made for wool or soap flakes, adding only the recommended amount to the washing water. Make sure the bowl is large enough to take the garment comfortably and wash only one garment at a time. Half fill the bowl with hot water and dissolve the detergent completely. Add enough cold water to make the water hand-hot and to cover the garment completely. The actual washing process should take as short a time as possible. Never leave knitwear to soak. Squeeze the garment gently in the warm suds to release the dirt. Turn it over, supporting it with both hands.

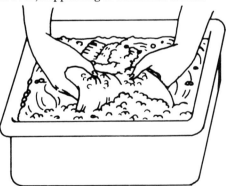

RINSING
Use plenty of water for rinsing, applying the same gentleness of touch as to the washing process. The rinsing water should be the same temperature as the washing water and there should be plenty of room for the garment to circulate freely. To make sure every trace of soap has been completely removed, rinse the garment several times in fresh water. Fabric conditioner can be added to the last rinse. Squeeze out the excess water. Do not wring.

DRYING
Roll the garment up in a thick clean towel to remove as much of the remaining water as possible.

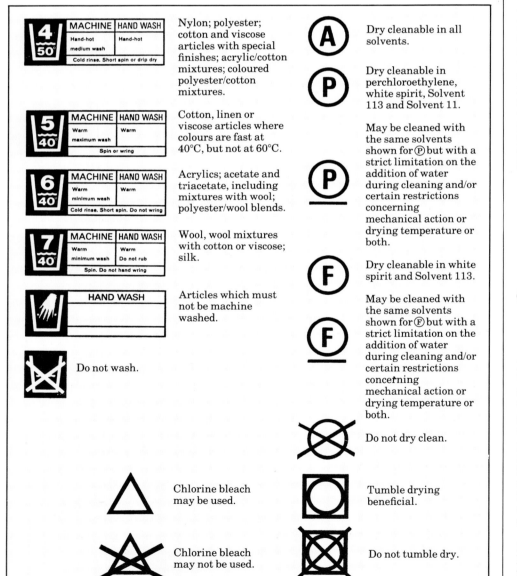

	MACHINE	HAND WASH	
4 / **50**	Hand-hot medium wash	Hand-hot	Cold rinse. Short spin or drip dry

Nylon; polyester; cotton and viscose articles with special finishes; acrylic/cotton mixtures; coloured polyester/cotton mixtures.

	MACHINE	HAND WASH	
5 / **40**	Warm maximum wash	Warm	Spin or wring

Cotton, linen or viscose articles where colours are fast at 40°C, but not at 60°C.

	MACHINE	HAND WASH	
6 / **40**	Warm minimum wash	Warm	Cold rinse. Short spin. Do not wring

Acrylics; acetate and triacetate, including mixtures with wool; polyester/wool blends.

	MACHINE	HAND WASH	
7 / **40**	Warm minimum wash	Warm Do not rub	Spin. Do not hand wring

Wool, wool mixtures with cotton or viscose; silk.

	HAND WASH	

Articles which must not be machine washed.

Do not wash.

△ Chlorine bleach may be used.

△(crossed out) Chlorine bleach may not be used.

Ⓐ Dry cleanable in all solvents.

Ⓟ Dry cleanable in perchloroethylene, white spirit, Solvent 113 and Solvent 11.

Ⓟ (underlined) May be cleaned with the same solvents shown for Ⓟ but with a strict limitation on the addition of water during cleaning and/or certain restrictions concerning mechanical action or drying temperature or both.

Ⓕ Dry cleanable in white spirit and Solvent 113.

Ⓕ (underlined) May be cleaned with the same solvents shown for Ⓕ but with a strict limitation on the addition of water during cleaning and/or certain restrictions concerning mechanical action or drying temperature or both.

⊗ Do not dry clean.

▢ Tumble drying beneficial.

⊠ Do not tumble dry.

Alternatively, spin it briefly if a drier is available. Do not use a tumble drier especially if the yarn contains synthetic fibres subject to heat damage. Complete the drying process with the garment laid flat and eased into shape on a dry towel, away from sunlight or any direct source of heat. Leave it until it is completely dry. Store in a clean dry drawer. Protect natural fibres with mothballs.

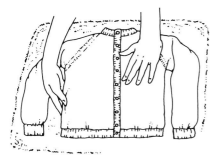

PILLING
After a while some garments become affected by 'pilling', where small balls of loose fibres form on the surface of the fabric. This effect can be minimised by washing garments inside out. To remove the pills, either pull them off or cut them off with a razor blade or sharp scissors.

SNAGGING
It's almost impossible not to snag knitwear at sometime or other. Sometimes a whole row of stitches can be tightened up in this way. Using the point of a knitting needle and beginning at the snag, gradually ease the stitches back to the correct size. Push any remaining slack to the back of the work. Cut the loop and darn in the loose ends.

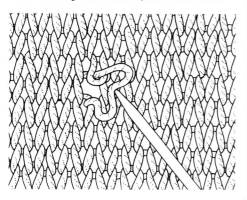

REPAIRING KNITWEAR
Some predictable repairs can be prevented during the making of a garment. Ribbed edges, for example, are subject to a great deal of wear and tear. To strengthen the edge cast it on or off using a double thickness of yarn. Some parts of a garment, elbows, for example, often wear thin after a while. These can be reinforced by Swiss darning.

Small holes can be repaired by rebuilding the stitches either by grafting, if only one row is affected, or by darning as shown. Large holes can be patched, either with knitted patches or, if it can be done decoratively, with patches made of leather or fabric.

Where the damage is extensive it may be necessary to reknit whole sections of the garment. Ribbed neckbands can easily be unravelled back to the main body of the garment. Reknit them either

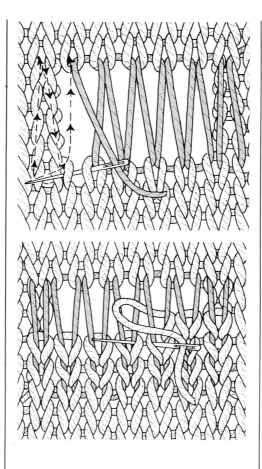

in the same or a contrast colour. It is also possible to reknit ribbed edges where they form the cast-on edge of the garment as is often the case on sleeves and sweater fronts and backs. Unpick the relevant seams, either the sleeve seam or the side seams, and pull a thread just above the point where the rib ends. Cut the yarn and, using a knitting needle, ease the stitches apart all along that row, removing the original yarn as you go. Pick up the stitches along the upper edge of the gap and reknit the rib downwards, following the original instructions but decreasing rather than increasing and *vice versa*.

ALTERATIONS
While it is quite impractical to alter the width of knitted garments, alterations to the length are relatively easy. Simply pull a thread as given above, pick up the stitches on either side of the gap and add as many rows as required. Finally graft the stitches on each side of the gap together. To shorten a garment, unravel as many rows as required before grafting the two sets of stitches together. Any added length can be worked either in the original yarn, if there is any left, or in one or more contrast colours. Make sure the stripes are at the same level on the back and front.

ADAPTING KNITWEAR
By combining the techniques for repairing and altering knitwear it is possible to give a well-worn garment a new lease of life with some simple adaptations. A plain round-necked sweater can be striped and given contrasting welts, for example. Make it into a slipover by removing the sleeves and adding armbands. Any garment

knitted in stocking stitch can be brightened up with some Swiss-darned motifs or patterns. Change the shape of a collar or the length of a sleeve. Shorten a dress into a sweater or a coat into a cardigan. When remodelling knitwear it is even possible to cut the fabric if you work two rows of machine stitching on each side of the proposed cut.

RECYCLING YARN
Clothes which are quite literally beyond repair, alteration or adaptation can, in some circumstances, be recycled. One of the advantages of hand-knitting is that the yarn from unsuccessful or discarded garments can often be unravelled, reconstituted virtually in its original form and re-used for something else. The effectiveness of this operation depends largely on the type of yarn, how long it has been knitted up and how well it has been cared for during that time. Heavily felted garments cannot be unravelled. Throw them away or use them for rag rugs. It is also difficult to unravel textured yarns like bouclé or hairy ones like mohair and angora. Cotton yarns tend to become unattractively stringy when unravelled as do many synthetics. The best chances of success are provided by plain good-quality woollen yarns. These can be unravelled in reasonably good condition several years after they were originally knitted up.

Having decided that the garment in question is a suitable candidate for recycling, unpick all the seams in reverse order to the original making up. Resist the temptation to cut seams or you will be left with lots of short lengths. When the garment has been dismantled, taking each section in turn, loosen the last stitch in the cast-off edge and thread the end of the yarn through it. Pull on the end to unravel the yarn. Wind it into loose hanks as you unravel. Tie the hanks in several places to prevent tangling. Inevitably, the yarn will be crinkly and it must be straightened before it can be reknitted. Either steam the yarn gently in the steam from a boiling kettle or wash it and dry it as described earlier for garments. When the yarn is completely dry, rewind it in balls ready for reknitting.

Original Yarns

For those who are able to obtain them, the following list describes the yarns originally used to knit up the garments on pages 8–113. Most of them are from French spinners or shops, whose yarns are available in the UK and USA only on a limited basis. The addresses of the appropriate agents, where they exist, are also given and readers may write to them for lists of stockists.

page 8
Georges Picaud California

page 10
Anny Blatt Flirt'Anny

page 12
Anny Blatt Écoss'Anny

page 14
Phildar Transat

page 18
Phildar Transat (used double)

page 20
Bouton d'Or Cordonnet

page 22
Welcomme Akala

page 24
Chat Botté Pétrouchka

page 26
Yves Saint Laurent Carina

page 28
Anny Blatt Flirt'Anny

page 30
Anny Blatt Pearl'Anny

page 32
Georges Picaud Zig

page 34
Anny Blatt Pearl'Anny

page 37
Chat Botté Nomades

page 40
Dorothée Bis Nostalgie

page 42
Berger du Nord Coton No 3

page 44
Phildar Tricot Phil

page 46
Bouton d'Or Soie

page 48
Bouton d'Or Cordonnet

page 50
Berger du Nord Tissé

page 52
Anny Blatt Flirt'Anny

page 54
Georges Picaud Série Noire

page 56
Bouton d'Or Confort

page 58
Anny Blatt No 4

page 60
Marigold 4-ply

page 62
Anny Blatt Angor'Anny

page 64
Berger du Nord Classique

page 66
Anny Blatt Sport'Anny

page 68
Georges Picaud Alpaga (used double)

page 70
Anny Blatt No 4

page 72
Berger du Nord Angora

page 74
Bouton d'Or Étoilé (used double)

page 76
Anny Blatt No 4

page 78
Bergère de France Jaspée (A)
Bergère de France Sport (B,C)

page 80
Anny Blatt Mohair et Soie (A,B)
Anny Blatt Tweed'Anny (C)

page 83
Pingouin Tricotine

page 86
Welcomme Maxi Mohair

page 88
Anny Blatt No 4

page 90
Yves Saint Laurent Carina

page 92
Berger du Nord Kid Mohair

page 94
Berger du Nord Lin d'Hiver

page 96
Anny Blatt No 4

page 98
Filatures de Paris 217 (used treble) (A)
Filatures de Paris Fleur de Laine (B,C,D)

page 100
Bergère de France Jaspée

page 102
Pingouin Mohair 50 (A,C)
Pingouin Vrillés (B)

page 104
Bouton d'Or Confort

page 106
Georges Picaud Alpaga

page 108
Anny Blatt Sport

page 111
Marigold Douceur

ADDRESSES

Anny Blatt
Ries Wools
242 High Holborn
London WC1
UK

Anny Blatt
24770 Crestview Court
Farmington
MI 01887
USA

Berger du Nord
Viking Wools
Rothay Holme
Rothay Road
Ambleside
Cumbria LA22 0HQ
UK

Berger du Nord
Bookman & Sons Inc
4872 NE 12th Avenue
Fort Lauderdale
FL 33334
USA

Chat Botté
Grove of Thame
Lupton Road Industrial Estate
Thame
Oxfordshire OX9 3RR
UK

Phildar (UK) Ltd
4 Gambrel Road
Westgate Industrial Estate
Northampton
UK

Phildar Inc
6438 Dawson Boulevard
Norcross
GA 30093
USA

Georges Picaud
Priory Yarns
24 Prospect Road
Ossett
West Yorkshire WF5 8AE
UK

Georges Picaud
Merino Yarn Co
230 Fifth Avenue
New York
NY 10001
USA

Pingouin
French Wools
7–11 Lexington
London W1
UK

Pingouin
PO Box 100
Highway 45
Jamestown
SC 29453
USA

Yves Saint Laurent
Trois Suisses
Marlborough House
38 Welford Road
Leicester LE2 7AA
UK